W9-BMT-995

Baby's Room

Baby's Room

Ideas and Projects for Nurseries

by Jessica Strand

Photographs by Jennifer Lévy

CHRONICLE BOOKS

SAN FRANCISCO

Library of Congress Cataloging-in-Publication Data:

Strand, Jessica.
    Baby's Room : ideas and projects for nurseries / by Jessica Strand;
    photographs by Jennifer Lévy.
    p. cm.
    Includes index.
    ISBN 0-8118-3293-7
    1. Nurseries. 2. Interior decoration. I. Lévy, Jennifer. II. Title.
    NK2117.N87 S77 2002

Manufactured in China

Designed by Deborah Bowman
Typeset by Deborah Bowman
Styling by Joanna Welliver and Lauren Hunter

Distributed in Canada by Raincoast Books
9050 Shaughnessy Street
Vancouver, British Columbia V6P 6E5

10 9 8 7 6 5 4 3 2 1

Chronicle Books LLC
85 Second Street
San Francisco, California 94105

www.chroniclebooks.com

dedication: To Stephen, who helped me build the nest, and to Lucian for filling it so beautifully.

acknowledgments

There are so many wonderful, generous people to thank for helping to make this book become a reality. First off, I'd like to thank all the families who let us into their beautiful homes and nurseries. I'd also like to thank all those who lent props, furniture, and linens—especially Mortise and Tenon, Ozzie and Moosey, and Garnet Hill. A big thanks and much gratitude to the team at Chronicle Books whose thoughts, direction, and input helped to shape this book. Thank you for your brilliance, Leslie Jonath, Jodi Davis, Ann Spivak, Jan Hughes, and Azi Rad. Many thanks to Jennifer Lévy, who gave life to my words with her lovely photographs, and to Sasha Emerson for her support, talents, and help. Deep appreciation and affection to Joanna Welliver for all her hard work, creative whimsy, and dedication to this project. Many thanks, as always, to my agent, Gail Hochman. Last but not least, a big thanks to my patient, loving husband, Stephen, for all his help and support.

contents

REAL NURSERIES

PROJECTS

introduction

When I began writing this book, I knew how excited I had been about putting together my son's room, but couldn't pinpoint exactly what made his finished nursery feel just right. As I interviewed families about their nurseries, what popped up each time were the personal touches that made each room stand out. All of the nurseries in this book include objects that reflect the family's personality, from a homemade floral hat rack to a re-invented chandelier to a 1948 Bozo record album and book found at a flea market. I realized while writing that my husband's bold paint job on the drawers in our son's room and my great-grandmother's quilt hanging on the wall were the extras that gave the space its own special, homey look. These meaningful items brought the room together.

A wonderful nursery can be any size or color, and can be decorated with hand-me-downs, thrift-store finds, pieces you've coveted in furniture or baby stores, or a combination of all of them. The perfect room for your child has absolutely nothing to do with how much money you spend; instead, the best nurseries show a personal stamp of love and warmth. The personality is dictated by your taste, passion, and spirit.

My hope is that this book will inspire, encourage, and help you to create a room that reflects your family and your child. I've organized it so that the front part of the book guides you through selecting each part of your nursery, from crib and changing table to floor and window treatments. I've tried to give you an idea of the many options available as well as the benefits of each alternative. Because safety is your first concern, I've listed issues to consider and precautions to take while you're decorating. The second part of the book shows specific nurseries, each with its own particular style and budget. You will hear the stories behind these rooms from the families who created them.

As a final note, you may well find that you're never truly finished decorating your nursery. As our children grow, becoming more active and independent, their rooms change to fit their lives. I've seen this firsthand with my son's room, which keeps evolving. I've taken pictures down and replaced them with a small wall cabinet to store objects out of his reach. I've bought bold-colored sheets, added a bureau with colorful painted knobs, and numerous baskets to hold his ever-expanding toy collection.

Enjoy this fun, exciting process, because this may be the most joyful and meaningful decorating project you'll ever do—as well as the last time you'll have this much control over your child's room.

the elements

The first step in planning a nursery is to really look at your space. Sit on the floor, walk around, look at the light at different times of the day—spend time in the room before you begin transforming. Ideas will spring up based on the room's integral shape, size, and character; you'll avoid mistakes by first combining the nursery of your imagination with the "reality" of the space. Let the room's size and shape help you to define your choices; obviously, what's good for a large space is not always going to work for a tiny one. Make sure to measure the room and take those numbers with you when you go shopping for anything for your nursery. Think about storage (Is there adequate storage in the room as is? Or will you want to build in storage, or need to budget for large shelving or drawer units? Or do you just need a few stacking boxes?) and light (Are there lots of windows, so that window treatments will inevitably be a major element in the decorating scheme? Or is it a dark room calling for a color palette and details that provide a sense of light and warmth?) before you begin purchasing or borrowing your furnishings.

It may be easier and less overwhelming if you mentally organize various nursery items into two categories: necessities and personal touches. The necessities, like bedding, lighting, window dressings, and floor coverings, make up the room. The personal touches—a family quilt, a homemade mobile, pictures of or by family members—give the room its warmth and unique flair.

All the items that you borrow or purchase for your nursery should be child-safe and serve their purpose for as long as your child is in diapers. Steer clear of furniture or accessories with small pieces, dangling strings, sharp edges, or parts that can be easily dismantled by small hands. Read the special sections in the first half of the book carefully for important reminders and tips for safety.

THEME AND COLOR

Many parents begin a nursery with either a theme, which could be as simple as decorating with animal images or objects, or a color palette, such as deciding that you want to use blue and white stripes throughout the room.

I began my nursery with two or three meaningful objects and these helped to guide my choices throughout the process.

In Camille's nursery, featured in the gallery of rooms in the second part of this book, her mother, Christina, used bold pink as the backdrop for her swinging Bohemian room. In Eamonn's nursery, woodcuts made by his grandfather inspired his parents to create a room that feels like a cabin in the woods.

The theme and color choices you make set the room's mood. Think of the airiness of a room filled with butterfly-inspired prints. Imagine how soothing

This delightful canopy was inspired by a circus tent in one of the pictures hanging on the wall.

and tranquil a room filled with pale greens and yellows can be. Picture the strong, energetic feel to a room decorated with airplanes and trucks in bold blues and reds.

Try new things. Be open-minded and throw conventions aside; you may surprise yourself with your choices. What you may have considered too bright, too subtle, too boyish or girlish for other rooms in your home might end up working perfectly in your nursery.

PAINT SHOPPING Before purchasing paint, gather paint chips from hardware or paint stores. If you like a particular color, look at various brands; usually each manufacturer has its own version with subtle differences.

Keep two things in mind when paint shopping. First, water-based paints are better than oil-based paints for several reasons: Because they are not as thick and sticky, they're easier to apply and dry more quickly, and they have less of a smell. Second, choose a paint finish that can be easily wiped off, such as a semigloss or washable eggshell finish: When your child becomes a toddler, those small hands will touch your walls every day.

The red crib adds striking contrast to the muted yellow walls of the nursery.

Safety Tips

- If you are pregnant, painting should be the job of another family member or a professional. The chemicals and fumes are not good for you or the unborn child.

- Be cautious if your house was built before 1978, when lead paint was banned. Lead poisoning is dangerous for everyone in the house. There are professionals in every major city who can help you detect problems, or you can buy a home detection kit at most hardware stores across the country. For more information, contact the National Lead Information Center, (800) 532-3394.

- Remember to paint the nursery at least a month before the arrival of the baby, so the room can ventilate properly. There shouldn't be a trace of paint smell when you move your new baby into the room.

THE CRIB

When we think of a baby's room, the first thing that comes to mind for most of us is the crib. More than any other piece of furniture, the crib symbolizes babyhood. When choosing a crib, the most important things to keep in mind are safety and comfort. Then you want to make it as inviting and cozy as possible.

Note: For the first several months many parents choose to use a bassinet or sidecar in their bedroom before settling their baby in a crib. Other parents follow the family-bed method for the first year. You may not need a crib immediately, but in most cases, sooner or later you'll be looking for or borrowing a crib that fits the rest of your nursery.

The bowed line of this crib's headboard and footboard give it the look of a sleigh bed.

STARTING YOUR CRIB SEARCH

Because there are so many types of crib, one can quickly get lost during the selection process. As with any furniture, you can choose extravagance or stick with the basics. While researching, I found a fifties-style round metal crib decorated with pleather and denim, as well as a standard metal crib with ostrich feathers attached to the posts. Both of these cost well over several thousand dollars apiece and made definitive statements. Keep in mind that you can find cribs decorated in organza and silk flowers or you can go with a simple spindle crib painted white—both function equally well and both please particular kinds of taste.

When you begin your search, try to look at many different styles before setting your sights on an individual crib. If you have friends with children, look at their cribs, pepper them with questions about their choice, and, most importantly, ask if they're happy with it. Gather as much information as you can before you go into the marketplace. Salespeople are persuasive. Don't be pushed into buying until you're sure it's just right. It's helpful to look through magazines, surf Web sites where they have photos and descriptions, order catalogs from baby stores, and, of course, window shop. If you get a sense of what's out there, it should help you to assess your needs as well as sharpen your idea of what kind of crib you want in your nursery.

There are four basic types of crib: standard cribs, convertible cribs, round cribs, and custom cribs. Within each category you'll find varying styles such as sleigh, canopy, spindle, French curve, Americana, Farmhouse, picket fence, Victorian, and Edwardian, just to name a few. You can also select from a wide range of materials ranging from brass to oak. But before looking at the details, let's see the benefits of each type of crib. If you opt for a hand-me-down, make sure your crib adheres to U.S. consumer standards. (See page 27 for more information.)

STANDARD CRIBS

A standard crib serves as a crib and only a crib. This type functions as a sleeping place for your child until they're two or three years old, depending on when your child makes the transition to a bed.

Most of the cribs available are standard cribs, so it's here that you will find the biggest range of styles. Also, since this is the most basic of crib styles, generally they are the least expensive. The disadvantage of a standard crib is that there's no way to "recycle" it when your child moves to a bed.

CONVERTIBLE CRIBS

A convertible crib converts into another type of furniture and often can convert to more than one piece. Some convertible cribs become youth beds and then transform into full-size beds; others become a daybed. Some have pieces which, when removed, can serve as a headboard for a full-size bed. The configurations vary widely.

When you buy this type of crib, although it's typically more expensive, you probably will not require another bed for your child for years. In some cases, if your child is obliging, you may never have to buy another bed for them at all. Of course, the notion of making such a long-term decision for your child before you've even set eyes on them may feel daunting. But if you like the design, it could be the best furniture purchase you'll make. And when you've converted it into a full-size bed, you don't have to use it in your child's room; there may be just the place for it elsewhere in your home.

Cribs are often the focal point of the nursery.

The Transition from Crib to Bed

Your child's transition to a real bed can begin at as early as two years; by three years most children have made the switch. Often you make the change when your child begins trying to climb or bounce out of their crib; literally the crib begins to feel too confining to them.

During the intermediary stage, put the crib mattress at its lowest level. You might want to take off the adjustable railing (this is feasible with most cribs) and put up your own guardrail. You'll find flexible guardrails at most baby stores.

Many guardrails for beds are made of mesh in a metal or wood frame and fold down so that you can put your child into the bed and then fold it back into the up right position after they're safely tucked in. They're most often set in place by securing a part of the frame beneath the mattress and box springs.

When you decide it's time to shop for a "big kid's bed," involve your child—you can even make it a family outing. Children love feeling included and feel very grown up when their input is considered, which can help ease the transition.

TOOLS

- tape measure
- pencil
- drill
- sewing machine or
  needle and thread

MATERIALS

- casement bracket,
  18-inch, metal
- plastic or butterfly anchors
  (see note)
- 10 yards fabric, 54 inches wide

project: **Crib Canopy**

Find the perfect spot for your child's crib and place this lovely, whimsical canopy over it. Not only will you jazz up the crib, but eventually you can use it elsewhere as a sweet little tented nook for your child.

1 Using the tape measure, find the center point of the crib.

2 Measure 83 inches from the floor. (This is a common canopy height; you may make it higher or lower as desired.) Hold the casement bracket at this point on the wall and mark with pencil. This is where the anchors will be fixed to the wall. Make sure to center the bracket above the crib before you attach it.

3 Using the drill, make holes in the wall for the anchors.

4 Fix the casement bracket to the wall with the anchors. Test the mounting by applying a little pressure. It should stay fixed to the wall.

5 Fold the fabric in half, narrow ends together. By machine or by hand, sew a 2-inch seam across the folded top. Pull the fabric to create a ruffle. Depending on how rough your selvages are, you may or may not want to finish them. However, your bottom edges should be finished.

6 Cover the bracket with the ruffle and arrange the canopy as you like: cascading over the crib, pulled to the side, or tied to the crib with ribbons made from the canopy fabric remnants.

Note: Purchase anchors that work with your particular wall type; for example, plaster, Sheetrock, wood paneling, and so on.

A crib canopy is perfect for a very small infant, but not something to keep when your child begins to sit up.

ROUND CRIBS

Round cribs are generally expensive and can be quite opulent. They look like a small wishing well in appearance and are often made of metals, although they do come in wood. There is no significant benefit to the round shape. For those who respond to this particular shape, there are a myriad of styles.

Because these cribs are unusual and costly, they tend to be more heavily designed. Very often they have themes, such as a "fairy tale" crib draped in deep green organza with dried flowers scattered over the sheer draping, or a "Louis XIV," a burnished gold-colored crib fitted with rich velvet bedding and drapery. These cribs are impressive and novel.

Not many stores sell these cribs, although they are readily available over the Internet. If you buy a round crib, purchase the mattress and bedding at the same time; since not many places offer them; accordingly, your choice in bedding will be somewhat limited.

CUSTOM CRIBS

A custom crib can refer to several things. It could mean that you've found a carpenter or store that will build a crib that you've designed yourself, or that you're altering an existing crib to your own specifications. Customizing may have nothing to do with the structure and everything to do with the finishing touches, such as decorative painting, the use of a particular theme, or creating effects such as a "distressed" look with special paints and stains.

Many stores and companies will modify, paint, or decorate a crib for an additional fee. If you don't have a variety of baby furniture or unfinished furniture stores available in your area, use the Internet to find the many companies that provide services in customizing cribs.

If you're having a crib built, you must follow particular guidelines so that the crib adheres to U.S. consumer product safety standards (see the sidebar on crib safety, page 27). If painting or decorating a crib yourself, it's imperative that the paint be lead free. Glued or hanging trinkets are not recommended by the Federal Safety Standards or the American Academy of Pediatrics.

OPPOSITE, TOP: This beautiful crib converts into a youth bed, which means it will be used for years.

OPPOSITE, BOTTOM: The sweet, hand-embroidered quilt adds a personal, family touch to the crib.

THE MATTRESS

Choosing a comfortable mattress that fits your crib snugly is as important as selecting a crib. You'll find a large selection of brands all offering varying qualities of mattresses.

The quality depends on a variety of things. The weight of the mattress in an indicator of how sturdy it is—if it's as light as a feather, then you know it's not the mattress for you. The mattress should have multiple inner springs, also called cadge coils. These metal coils help to make the mattress firmer. The coils are wrapped in polyfiber, coconut fiber, or cotton covering. Well-made mattresses usually have two types of padding over the springs; for example, coconut fiber with a quilted cotton covering. This lends cushioning and comfort to the firmness provided by the inner spring.

As with the crib search, there are specific safety standards that you must be aware of and follow for your child's well being when choosing a mattress. These guidelines are listed on page 27.

If you are borrowing a crib, consider investing in a new mattress. A mattress that has had less wear and tear gives a whole new feeling to the crib and lets you know the type, age, and quality of your mattress. You'll know that the mattress your baby sleeps on was not sitting in someone's garage absorbing the odors of oil and gasoline. You'll feel more relaxed and confident about your choices when you have complete knowledge about the furnishings for your baby's room.

the elements

BEDDING

"Bedding" refers to sheets, pillows, blankets, dust ruffles, quilts, and the bumper—all the bed linens you use to make up your child's crib.

The bumper is a soft padded cushion that you tie around the crib's interior to create a shield from the bars of the crib as your baby moves around. Typically bumpers are secured to the sides of the crib with short pieces of fabric. These ties should be just long enough to fix in a knot or bow, but not long enough to pose a choking hazard to your child.

Many people remove the bumper when the baby begins to sit or pull up at around five or six months. They're concerned that the bumper may help children climb out of the crib. However, I know many mothers, myself included, who leave the bumper on because their children like the soft padding and don't seem to use the bumper as a step up for climbing. This depends on your child's personality; always err on the side of caution and remove the bumper if you sense your child is a climber.

Outfitting a crib is simple. You won't need more than a bumper, a bottom sheet, and several light blankets or a quilt. Note: Experts advise that you never put pillows or toys in the crib with your baby. Scatter decorative or ornamental pillows in your nursery if you like, but the crib should be a clean, object-free sanctuary where your child sleeps.

As you explore your options, you'll find a full range of possibilities since all of these items come in different fabrics, patterns, and designs. The prices range considerably as well; as with any item, you can take a cost-efficient approach or an expensive one.

There are multiple catalogs, Web sites, and baby stores that sell the simplest bedding solutions to the most elaborate (see the resources listed at the back of this book). The more upscale baby furniture stores have multiple fabrics on hand and have connections to sources that make custom bedding, but this route can be quite expensive. Interior designer Sasha Emerson suggests another way to create your own look without spending too much: "I often look through bargain bins at fabric stores and bring materials to my favorite seamstress, who'll sew it for half the price." If you're a good seamstress, there are patterns available to make your own bumper, dust ruffle, and sheets.

The bedding choices you make are integral to the nursery and often affect other choices you make for the room. If bedding is one of the first things you choose, the window treatments, floor covering, paint color, and decorative touches can all be affected.

There is such a variety out there that the ideal bedding for your nursery is within reach. Read the tips on the facing page to help you avoid feeling overwhelmed. Try to be as open-minded as you can about your choices. You can mix and match patterns and colors. You may purchase a bumper at one place

OPPOSITE, TOP: A mix of old and new—the patterned fabric is vintage, the striped material is new—adds a bold, playful touch to this nursery.

OPPOSITE, BOTTOM: Bolder, more theme-driven bedding, like this nautical bumper, carry out a nursery's motif.

Good Things to Look for in Bedding

Softness: Any fabric that touches your baby's skin should be soft and free of scratchy seams. It's better to look for natural fabrics like 100-percent cotton, which is less likely to cause any kind of skin irritation or reaction.

Livable Patterns: If you choose a patterned fabric, find one you won't tire of. While subdued colors are often associated with babies, bright colors and bold patterns have been found to stimulate early brain development. So there's no need to shy away from them.

Baby-Proof Decorations: Pom-poms, fringe, and bows can all pose a choking hazard if your baby pulls them off bedding. Choose bedding that you're certain is baby-proof.

Anchor · Buoy · Oars · Life buoy · Sea gull · Ship's Wheel · Anchor · Oars · Life buoy

and the sheets somewhere else. And remember, you can always change your mind. Sometimes all it takes is a different set of sheets to transform the "old" look into a "new" look. Don't feel pressured by family, friends, or anyone who feeds you rules about decorating your child's room. There is no prescribed way of decorating. The only imperative consideration is safety; beyond that, anything goes.

CLOCKWISE FROM TOP LEFT: Yellow and blue contrast nicely and work equally well for a boy or a girl.

A simple change of a blanket can transform the look of your nursery.

Finding bedding that you like is often the first step in planning a nursery.

Safety Tips

- Crib slats should be no more than $2\frac{3}{8}$ inches apart according to Federal Safety Standards, Industry Voluntary Standards, and the American Academy of Pediatrics. Any crib made before 1991 should be checked, because safety standards have changed since then.

- The U.S. Consumer Product Commission wants consumers to beware of crib posts that extend above the top of the crib by more than $\frac{1}{16}$ of an inch. You'll want to get rid of these—but you don't necessarily have to toss the entire crib. You may be able to unscrew some extensions, while others will have to be sawed off and sanded until they're smooth. Most manufacturers have discontinued cribs with extensions, but if you are using an older crib, check the posts. You don't want your child banging or catching themselves on them.

- All joints and parts should fit tightly and the wood should be splinter free.

- Make sure the paint is lead free and that it's not peeling or cracking.

- When lowered, the crib sides should be at least 9 inches above the mattress so that the baby doesn't fall out. When the sides are raised they should be at least 26 inches above the mattress support in its lowest position.

- The drop side should have a locking, hand-operated latch that will not release accidentally.

- The mattress should fit snugly, eliminating any chance of the baby getting any part of their body stuck between the mattress and the crib slats. If two fingers fit between the mattress and the crib, the mattress is too small.

- Always check the length and size of bumper cords; they are necessary, but you don't want them to be so long that they are choking hazards.

- Remember to always remove pillows, fluffy blankets or comforters, and stuffed animals or toys from the crib before you put your baby down to sleep. Because newborns are not able to turn their heads, these items may pose a suffocation risk. Some experts believe that sleeping on too soft a surface may increase the chance of SIDS (Sudden Infant Death Syndrome), so make sure your baby's mattress is flat and firm. If you choose to use a bumper, take care that it is securely fastened to the crib.

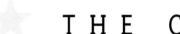

THE CHANGING TABLE

My changing table was the purchase I was least happy with. I bought a changing table—not a bureau, not a cabinet, but an open, freestanding changing table that was lovely for the first seven months and then became obsolete. Little did I know that my child would love to pull the diapers, burpies, blankets, wipes, anything and everything off the shelves. By the time he was ten months old, I was looking for a bureau to replace it. If I had known more about the options out there and had realized how quickly an infant becomes a mobile toddler I would have made a different decision.

You want a changing table that is sturdy, self-contained, and that holds all your various diapering necessities. There are a lot of options that fit those requirements, as you'll see here.

THE CLASSIC CHANGING TABLE

There are many classic styles of changing tables. All of them have a flat surface where you can place a changing pad. Some are open with shelves on the bottom, some look like small cabinets, and others come with large decorative baskets where you can store your diapers, burpies, etc. Each of these styles serves its own function, but do choose a table that serves your needs when your child is mobile as well as during infancy.

A classic freestanding changing table with shelves has space enough to store all the essentials—diapers, wipes, and lotions.

The "Found" Changing Table

With an open mind and a little ingenuity, you can fashion a one-of-a-kind changing table from any number of other furniture pieces. If you're interested in going this route, you'll start looking at furniture very differently. This funky approach may not be for you if you're leaning toward a more traditional nursery. But if you're happier with the unconventional, then start browsing for the perfect piece of furniture to turn into a changing table. Just keep these requirements in mind:

- A flat surface that's a comfortable height for dressing and undressing a child.
- An area to store diapers, cream, wipes, etc.
- The piece needs to be sturdy and shouldn't move or sway when you push against it.
- No sharp corners.

Obviously a cabinet with drawers or cupboards makes it difficult for a child to make any mischief once you've baby-proofed it. If you have your eye on an open changing table, think about getting baskets (to hold all changing essentials) that fit snugly into the shelves of the table, creating a kind of drawer. This will help to keep your changing supplies contained once your child is crawling and grasping.

BUREAU WITH CHANGING TOP

This popular changing table offers two benefits in one. It serves first as a changing table and then continues to be useful as a bureau long after your child is out of diapers. You just pull off the changing attachment and you can use the bureau in their room or in another room of your house.

This is also true of a bureau with a foam changing attachment. Some of the attachments have straps while others screw into the top of the bureau. This takes a little more assembling and may not be as pristine in appearance, but it is the less expensive option of the two.

A CHANGING TABLE THAT'S ALL YOURS

You can create a changing table from a wide variety of furniture. I've seen them adapted from a stainless steel kitchen cart, a butcher-block desk, and an old index-card file from a library. The great thing about this alternative is that you can always use the piece of furniture later in your home.

OPPOSITE, TOP: Any sturdy piece of furniture that's the right height can serve as a changing table. Here, a 1950s cabinet is transformed into a changing table with chic to spare.

OPPOSITE, BOTTOM: A butcher-block cart makes a great changing table; its shelves are perfect for storage.

ABOVE: This freestanding changing table uses baskets kept below to help with organization.

A changing pad transforms any flat, roomy, easily
accessible surface into a place to diaper your baby.

ONE COMFORTABLE CHAIR

When I began the task of choosing a chair for our nursery, almost all my friends and all the parenting magazines recommended a glider as the most comfortable option. I sat in what felt like a million of them, never fully convinced that they were more comfortable than any other chair. But the pressure to get the "right" chair for the nursery initially kept me from looking at the wide range of possibilities.

Finally, when I broadened my view, I found a chair that worked for me. I chose a comfortable wicker rocker with a high back and a deep seat. Even though I was pleased with my choice, I found myself defending it—"It's really comfortable, more comfortable than any glider I sat in." I realized that the glider had embodied all my anxieties and fears about becoming a parent. If I broke out and didn't get the "popular" item, I wasn't making the right decision for my child. Perhaps this is the first lesson to be learned in parenthood: Be confident about your choices. The chair I chose worked out beautifully.

A comfortable chair is a big part of making your nursery a haven. In this special chair, you'll watch the child in your arms grow both physically and emotionally. In the beginning, the chair will be a place where you nurse or bottle-feed your child. Eventually, it might be the chair where you read a story before bedtime.

Everyone has their theories about what works and what doesn't in a nursery: which chairs are the most soothing to the baby, the easiest to feed in, etc. However, from my own experience and from talking

An overstuffed chair and ottoman is comfortable for nursing now, and for bedtime stories in the years to come.

to other mothers, what matters more than anything else is that the chair be exceedingly comfortable to you. Here, we'll look at various "comfortable chairs" you might consider for your nursery.

GLIDERS

The classic glider is made out of wicker or wood and usually comes with a matching ottoman. Instead of rocking back and forth, you glide atop a stationary base. The smooth, even ride and lulling motion can help to relax the mother and the baby. Because the base never lifts from the floor, it keeps fingers, sleeves, toys, and animal tails from getting caught, as they can be under a rocker's runners. Also, the padding on a glider's armrests provides instant comfort and support to tired arms.

Most gliders are cushioned. If it's in your budget, you can choose the fabric to go along with the décor in your room. If you're going the less expensive route, there are plenty of attractive, reasonably priced chairs out there. You might have to assemble your glider and you will have a limited choice when it comes to fabrics and the color of the wood, but you may save several hundred dollars. The other cost-effective way to go is to look for floor or showroom sales at baby stores where the items are marked down considerably; you will have to take the glider home as is, but it may be the chair of your dreams.

ROCKERS

With over eighty styles of rocker to choose from, with names like Windsor, Amish, Mission, Craftsman, Shaker, Modern Scandinavian, Kennedy, Morris, and Shaker, just to list a few, it's difficult to make a choice. Start by sitting in as many different styles of chair as you can find.

Matt Bearson, owner of Rocking Chairs 100% in Marin County, California, says, "When you buy a rocking chair for a nursery, you should be thinking in the long term. You want to buy a chair that you're going to want to have as a memento. It's an 'instant heirloom' and one of the most unique pieces of gear for the nursery. You will be spending a significant amount of money, so buy something you love."

A good rocking chair has steam-bent components; essentially it's built to last. A well-made rocking chair also offers good lower back support. Because they're carefully balanced to ensure that they move evenly, it's important not to add too much padding to a chair that's not made for it. Placing a quilt or a throw over the top for more headrest support or using a small back pillow for lumbar support is fine, but when you begin to attach padding to every inch of the chair, you compromise its comfort and balance. You may want to place a pillow under your arm while you feed your baby. This will cushion the wooden arms and give you a little extra support.

Besides looking for the most comfortable chair, look for one that you can easily get in and out of. Matt Bearson steers mothers away from two particular chairs, the Bentwood and the Adirondack, which have seats too deep to get out of easily while holding a baby.

ABOVE: The classic glider provides an ideal setting in which to lull your baby and yourself to sleep.

RIGHT: A comfortable distressed white rocker with a colorful pillow adds rustic charm to the nursery.

OVERSTUFFED CHAIRS

Another alternative is a big overstuffed chair that gives your back enough support and lets your arms rest at a comfortable height. Though I had a rocker in my nursery, I sometimes nursed in the overstuffed chair in my living room. There was something about the cozy, enveloping feeling of the chair that made me relax—and the upholstered armrests worked perfectly for resting the crook of my arm.

For the first several months, every time you feed, you're holding the weight of your baby's head. It's a good idea to cushion your elbow area; an overstuffed chair does this without any extra effort from you.

There are plenty of styles of overstuffed chair that will work beautifully in a nursery. Just make sure that the armrest is comfortable for you. You can test this by putting your arms in the "holding baby" position (borrow a stuffed animal at the store) to see how it feels. You also might want to consider some kind of ottoman with this type of chair. There's something about the way one's body falls into the chair that begs for a place to rest your feet.

Inexpensive stools designed for nursing help both mother and baby relax at feeding time.

One disadvantage of this style is that "overstuffed" often means "oversized." If your nursery is small, this type of chair may take up too much room. If your nursery is large and the overstuffed option appeals to you, by all means splurge on a big, comfy chair.

FOOT SUPPORT

All of us feel better when we put our feet up at the end of a long day. But for a new mother who's up nights, carrying a child around all day, and constantly feeding, a foot support can really make a difference. Elevating your feet, according to breastfeeding experts, can also relieve strain on your back, neck, and shoulders during feedings.

Here are a few foot support options to consider and test for yourself.

GLIDER AND UPHOLSTERED OTTOMANS

A glider ottoman works exactly like a glider chair, moving back and forth on a stationary base. A standard upholstered ottoman is stationary. Both of these styles set your feet at the same level as the chair, taking your body weight completely off your legs. The upholstered or cushioned ottomans are soft yet sturdy and make sitting a pleasure.

The overstuffed chair I sat in most often while breastfeeding had a large overstuffed ottoman. The combination of the two made me want to sit there for hours at a time.

WOODEN AND PLASTIC NURSING STOOLS

An inexpensive option, simple footstools designed for nursing range in price from twenty-five to sixty-five dollars. The angled design helps to take the weight off your legs and feet while lifting your midsection, thus relaxing your abdomen and helping to support your lower back. All of this puts less pressure on your shoulders and arms, making feedings much easier on your entire body.

OTHER ALTERNATIVES FOR RESTING YOUR FEET You could also choose a foam or beanbag ottoman; these are less expensive than a glider, wicker, or stuffed ottoman and provide a good deal of comfort. They're available in lots of durable soft fabrics and can be found in numerous stores and catalogs. Note: If you use a beanbag, check its seams before your child begins crawling to be certain the filling doesn't leak. The best beanbags have an inner lining to ensure that they're baby-safe.

Of course, if a foot support simply isn't in the budget or you don't care for the look of a permanently residing ottoman in your decorating scheme, you can always pull over another chair or a side table with a pillow on it on which to raise your feet. Both of these work perfectly well. You just have to make sure that you have the space for more furniture, you don't want to be tripping over chairs and tables while you're busy comforting your child.

COZY EXTRAS

In addition to the comfortable chair, there are other pieces that can increase comfort while you're feeding your child, such as a side table, a single bed, a day bed, a lounge—pieces that make nursing easier while making your nursery cozy.

Some nurseries are big enough to accommodate a sofa. Throw pillows add colorful accents that can complement your décor.

SINGLE BED

If you have enough room in your nursery, a single bed is a wonderful idea. It gives you another place to settle with your baby to cuddle, comfort, rest, and feed. Particularly when they're very small and need to be fed every two or three hours, it's lovely to have a place where you can rest as well—and possibly even nap with them.

When the child becomes more mobile, you may not need the bed as much; at that point you can turn it into a couch by pushing it against a wall and adding bolsters and throw pillows. Or, of course, you can take the bed out of the room and use it elsewhere in the house.

SMALL TABLE OR CHEST

You're going to need a table or other surface to hold bottles, a lamp, a glass of water (you'll need to stay hydrated, particularly if you're breastfeeding), a book, a piece of toast, a diaper—the anything and everythings of caring for an infant.

You might want several surfaces for plunking stuff down, but have at least one in the nursery if you are going to feed your child there. Look for a surface that will work next to the nursing chair and make sure it's a comfortable height so you can easily grab things while you're in the midst of feeding.

PILLOWS

I never fully appreciated pillows until I was pregnant. I could place them here and there, manipulate them until they supported this or that part of my back, stomach, neck, calves, and feet. I even placed them between my legs at night; somehow the cushioning made for a better night's sleep.

After my son was born, I continued to use them. While you're feeding a tiny infant there's nothing more helpful than a lot of pillows to help support the baby, your arms, your back, all of you.

Some pillows are made specifically for certain purposes; several good candidates for chair-time with baby are discussed in the following pages. Each of these may work better than just regular old pillows for some people, while others may find the classic cushion all that they need. Always try out the pillows before purchasing them. What sounds good may not always feel good.

ABOVE: Boldly striped and patterned pillows give a room depth and color.

OPPOSITE: The colors of the overstuffed rocker, ottoman, and lime green throw pillow work well together.

NURSING PILLOW Nursing pillows help to take some of the pressure off your arms and back by lifting the baby closer to your breast so that you're not bending over or straining.

You have several shapes to choose from. One popular style is the donut-shaped nursing pillow; a well-known brand is the Boppy. Soft but slightly stiffer than your average pillow, it's about six to eight inches high and fits around your waist. Boppies are usually covered in a soft, heavy fabric like a brushed denim. Another style of nursing pillow is made of stiff foam, usually covered in flannel or terry cloth, that provides support by fitting into your lap. The "My Brest Friend Nursing Pillow," a wearable pillow with a padded back support, is covered in a soft durable fabric.

I experimented with several types of pillows and found that the one that fit around my waist was most helpful; I liked it because it stayed in place but was less stiff, so it was easier to manipulate. Many women I know also loved the "My Brest Friend Pillow," which helps make breastfeeding easier and eases back strain.

BACK PILLOW Back pillows come in all shapes and sizes and are stuffed with various fillers, from beans to synthetic fibers. These types of pillows are obviously not marketed solely to pregnant women or mothers with infants; they're available to anyone with a back problem, or to prevent aches and cramps.

Feeding your child, as wonderful and relaxing as it is, can be hard on your back. Because you are carrying a substantial weight and leaning over a good deal for the first year of your baby's life, any back support you use can provide relief.

Obviously, standard all-purpose pillows can help you get comfortable, but a pillow that's designed

ABOVE: A small pillow for your back can make you more comfortable while nursing.

TOOLS

- washing machine or sink
- cardboard, 30-inch square
- roller sponge
- rubber stamps
- sewing machine
- scissors

MATERIALS

- Rit liquid dye
- white cotton fabric, 25 inches by 14 inches
- color-fast paint
- 17-inch bolster pillow form
- 2-foot cotton or silk ribbon, 1½ inches wide

project: **Small Pink Bolster**

This bolster is not only a great decorative touch, it's also a nice size to use for lower back or arm support while you're nursing or feeding.

❶ Following the directions on the Rit bottle, fill your washing machine or sink with water and pour in the dye. (Note: Old porcelain sinks are apt to stain.) Add the fabric and allow to soak until it reaches the desired color. The darker you want it, the longer it should remain in the dye.

❷ Remove the fabric from the solution and wring well. Lay it flat on top of the cardboard so it doesn't stain the tabletop. Let dry completely.

❸ Using the roller sponge, lightly coat the rubber stamps with paint.

❹ Press the stamps firmly onto the fabric, positioning the images 1 to 2 inches apart. Let the paint dry completely.

❺ Fold the narrow ends of the fabric under, forming a ¼-inch hem, and sew in place with the sewing machine.

❻ Place the fabric printed-side down and fold in half horizontally. With the sewing machine, sew along the length of the fabric, forming a tube that's open at both ends.

❼ Turn the case printed-side out and slip the pillow form into the case, leaving an equal amount of fabric at each end.

❽ Cut 1-foot lengths of ribbon for each end of the pillow. Gather both ends and tie securely with the ribbons.

Note: These pillows are meant for adult use only; color-fast paint can be dangerous for babies.

the elements

45

solely to give you lumbar support may make a big difference in the long-term health of your back.

BABY LOUNGE-ROUND This large, cuddly pillow looks a bit like a dog bed for a Great Dane. It is particularly useful when your child becomes mobile; toddlers can roll, relax, and play on their own special cushioned island. It's also easy to move around the house, so it's as mobile as your child is. These fabulous pillows are available in a variety of fabrics, or you can have a custom cover made to match the décor of your nursery or playroom.

Joanna Welliver, the main stylist for this book, bought one for her child at around sixteen months. "He loves cozying up with me, with friends, or just by himself with a toy or book. My son loves to lie on the Lounge-Round just to stretch out and relax. He delights in the fact that it's just his size."

This Lounge-Round is a special place for a toddler to tumble, play with toys, read, or just rest.

48

★ LIGHTING

It's important to consider the light in your child's room. You want it to be cheery, but not to look like a hospital room. You want enough light to read and play by, and a little bit of light to check on your sleeping infant.

When choosing lamps, put safety first. Be especially cautious with floor lamps and halogen lamps.

CLOCKWISE FROM TOP LEFT: A labor of love, this hand-decorated lampshade gives a lamp its own unique look.

A painted wrought iron chandelier is both funky and feminine—just right for a little girl's room.

A quick coat of paint transforms a thrift-store find into clever, unusual lighting.

Use a standing lamp only if you secure it to the ground; mobile babies like to pull themselves up using anything handy and a standing lamp provides the perfect means. Halogen bulbs get extremely hot and are far too bright for a nursery.

OVERHEAD LIGHTING

Ceiling lights are the safest way to light your baby's room. If the existing ceiling lamp in your room isn't pretty or doesn't shed the kind of light that gives the room a warm glow, you can remedy this problem.

First, choose a relatively low-wattage lightbulb, then pick a shade or cover that creates a warmer light. Installing a dimmer switch in your nursery lets you control the level of light and easily check in without disturbing your child.

TABLE LAMPS

You'll find more variety in this type of lamp than any other. Don't limit yourself to lamps designed for nurseries. There are antique lamps with lovely delicate detailing, modern lamps with more angular lines, and Japanese Noguchi-style lamps that lend a playful feel to any room. I visited a beautiful nursery with an Art Noveau–style lamp with a multicolored glass shade in the shape of a snail.

You can choose a lamp that makes a statement of its own—playful, zany, dramatic—or find something that fits more demurely into the décor of your nursery. You can use a lamp to pick up the color of the walls, drapes, or linens or something in the theme of the room, like a sea horse, a lion, a cowboy, or a ballerina. Of course, you can always settle for a neutral lamp that simply provides the right amount of light.

See the Safety Tips at right for precautions to consider when using a table lamp.

SCONCES AND WALL FIXTURES

These fixtures combine the benefits of overhead lighting and table lamps. They give a softer light and are not as dangerous as table lamps, since there's no cord and they're not easily knocked over.

The ideal fixture is hard-wired into the wall so there are no cords or extraneous wires to take care of. If this isn't the case, try to place the fixture as close to the outlet as you can. Attach any loose cords to the wall with a cord cover or masking tape.

NIGHT-LIGHTS

Night-lights sound terrific in principle, but in practice they may be more trouble than they are worth in the nursery. Not only are night-lights tempting to toddlers (because many of them come in playful colors and designs), they are also controversial.

Studies done in the last several years suggest that there may be a correlation between a dim light in a baby's room and vision deficiencies in adults. Though none of the findings provide conclusive evidence that a night-light causes myopia later in life, you may want to play it safe and not use one.

 Safety Tips

- Make sure that there are no loose lamp cords anywhere that a toddler can grab.

- Gather cords and cover them with a cord cover or masking tape. Or use a small tack that fits around the cord, which you'll secure by hammering into the piece of furniture and then the wall.

- Halogen lamps get too hot and can cause severe burns.

- Floor lamps must be secured to the floor; it may be best not to use floor lamps while your child is a toddler.

CLOCKWISE FROM TOP LEFT: A paper lantern adds an Asian flair.

A vintage lamp with a fresh new shade combines the best of old and new.

A wall sconce is another good way to illuminate your baby's room.

★ WALLS

There are myriad ways to treat the walls in your baby's room. Whether they're a soft white, a colored backdrop, or the theme on which all else is based, you'll find the walls have a lot to do with how your nursery feels.

You may decide that a fresh coat of paint is the way to go, or you may decide to keep the room as is, but paint the molding or ceiling a different color. You can wallpaper or use stencils or stamps, and there's a limitless list of ideas for murals. Make it easy on yourself. Narrow it down to what's feasible, practical, and within your budget—and choose a wall treatment that your child won't grow out of too quickly.

This bold stencil of the moon and stars adds color and playfulness to the walls of the nursery.

WALLPAPER

Wallpaper can cover every inch of the walls or be used as a decorative border or trim. Choose paper that's durable and easy to clean. Both vinyl-backed and coated papers satisfy these requirements.

Wallpapering is a big undertaking. Of course, if you've done it before, then the intricacies of getting the paper to lie flat and the corners to meet won't be as daunting. If the task seems overwhelming, you can always use decorative paper just on borders or trim. If you're not handy or don't have much time but are sold on using wallpaper, then adjust your budget and hire a professional.

When you're ready to purchase, bring samples of the wallpapers you like with you. Also, be sure to measure the room very carefully to figure out how much wallpaper you'll need. Guessing can mean you'll waste money on rolls that you don't need.

PAINTED MURALS

There are many types of murals and many ways of doing them. You can hire a decorative painter to create a particular scene, character, or landscape you've conceived for the nursery. Or, if you've got talent with a paintbrush, you could undertake a mural yourself. Scenes for a mural can also be constructed with stencils.

Obviously, the route you take will determine the expense. Erin Arnold, a decorative artist, told me, "People often underestimate the length of time it takes to paint a mural. In some cases it takes a week, sometimes a month or two, so it's important to start this process early." Because they are so labor intensive, you want to be certain of your design. You'll want a mural that will excite your children's imagination, and amuse and soothe them for a good long time.

STAMPS AND STENCILS

Stamps and stencils are fun, inexpensive ways to decorate your walls, whether you're aiming for a whimsical or a finished look. Stamps come in a broad range of choices, from modern geometrical designs to antique floral images. You can find stamps at art stores, home decorating centers, upscale hardware stores, or shops specializing in stamps. (Check the resources at the back of the book.) If you're interested in designing your own stamp, draw a picture of the design and ask about specialists in your area at your local art supply store.

Although they take a patient hand, stamps are incredibly easy to apply. All you do is put the stamp impression into acrylic paint and press it to the wall. Before you begin pressing, sketch the design you wish to create. Even if you want to create a free-flowing look, a rough plan will save you time and any anxiety you might feel about the outcome.

Test the stamps before you begin. Try different colors of paint on a similar background before you stamp on your walls. You'll get a sense of which colors stand out best, and you'll be able to see if the stamp impressions are as clear as you had hoped.

Stenciling is another simple way of transforming a space. Whether you stencil a corner, a wall, borders or trim, this decorative technique adds old-fashioned charm to a room. Stencils are available at art stores, home centers, paint and hardware stores, and sometimes even at stationery shops. You can also make your own stencils by tracing a particular shape or design onto a piece of heavy paper and cutting it out.

Stenciling is a bit more labor intensive than stamping. First, you have to set the stencils where you want them, then you spray over the stencil with a latex paint or use a stencil brush to fill in the image. After you've allowed the paint to dry, just pull off the stencil.

If you are pregnant, you should not be near paint fumes, so recruit non-pregnant volunteers to stamp or stencil the walls. Also, allow at least a week for the room to air out before moving the baby into the nursery.

CLOCKWISE FROM TOP LEFT: The floral border adds a touch of whimsy to a softly painted room.

Traditional baby icons comprise this playful border.

Delicate wallpaper captures the soul of this serene nursery.

WINDOWS

When my husband and I traveled with our son to Italy, I thought the time change, a 20-hour flight, and jet lag would throw his schedule entirely off. But he quickly caught up on his sleep, and I'm convinced it was because the enormous window shutters so common in Italy blocked out all the light in our room. When we arrived home, we immediately bought a blackout shade, which has made a big difference in how well our son sleeps.

When you're considering window covers, take into account the light-blocking abilities of various styles. You can always combine treatments so light is blocked and you get the look you want. You could

Checkered trim gives these drapes and the valance a sunny outlook.

use a blackout shade and hang curtains or a Roman shade over it. Or you may be more partial to the look of blinds—just make sure that they block light. All of these choices come in many designs, colors, and materials, and even blackout shades can be decorative.

See the Safety Tips at the end of this section for precautions to take with window treatments.

CURTAINS

When buying curtains, measure your window carefully. Figure out where you'd like the curtain to hang from (it doesn't have to be right at the top of the window—it could be higher) and where you'd like it to fall to. Floor-length drapes are fine when your child is an infant but they soon become a liability. Not only can your child hang from the curtain and pull on it, it's also difficult to control the dust that gathers at the hem. A standard-length curtain that falls to the windowsill may make more sense.

Some fabrics you'd never expect in a nursery work wonderfully. Imagine a brilliantly colored silk linen that filters light, casting a colored glow over the room. Or consider how a rich velvet brocade can instantly add depth and warmth. If you start with a roller or blackout shade to block out the light, the sky's the limit as far as curtain fabric and design are concerned.

SHADES

A roller or blackout shade or blinds should be a staple in your nursery. They let you create an environment that accommodates your baby's sleep schedule.

Because a blackout shade has an extra layer that keeps light from penetrating, it's your best bet for keeping the room dark. Buy a shade that fits your window exactly or one just a tad bigger so light doesn't peek through.

A balloon or Roman shade tends to be more decorative than functional. Like curtains, they come in a variety of fabrics and designs. Because this type of shade is often made from sheer materials, getting a roller or blackout shade to go underneath your window treatment might be a good idea.

If you prefer a sleeker look, use a roller or blackout shade by itself in a fabric or color that matches your décor. You can make it distinctive by using a little trim on the bottom of the shade and/or an inventive, playful pull. Imagine a plain white shade with hand-stamped deep purple and red dinosaurs, red and purple rickrack at the bottom, and a pull made from a wooden dinosaur ornament. How about a pale violet and pink floral shade trimmed in old lace, with an oversized creamy vintage button attached. You can come up with a window covering that suits your style perfectly without spending a lot of money.

FOLDING SCREENS AND CURTAIN ROOM DIVIDERS

Folding screens can be both useful and decorative. They're a great way to divide a room if your children are sharing, or if you are using only part of a room as a nursery.

Screens are best when your child is not yet mobile, since most screens can be easily pulled down, knocked over, or damaged by a toddler. If you're set on a screen, make sure to secure it to the floor. You could turn a screen into a sort of sliding door by mounting it to a floor attachment available at high-end hardware stores. Or drill holes in the floor and the screen and bolt it to the floor.

Though not as sophisticated or chic as a foldaway screen, a curtain doesn't present as many potential problems. Once you have a curtain rod mounted to the ceiling, then all you need is a large curtain or two depending on the length of the space.

OPPOSITE, TOP: The clean lines of a roller shade may be the best bet if your nursery isn't the least bit fussy.

OPPOSITE, BOTTOM: Wooden blinds block out the light and give a room a warm, homey feel.

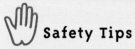 **Safety Tips**

- If you're using vinyl blinds, make sure they weren't made before 1996. Many of these contain lead.

- Keep curtain and drape cords out of your child's reach. You can buy hooks, place them high on the wall adjacent to the cords, and wind the cords tightly around the hooks. There are also child-proofing devices made specifically for this purpose; for example, you can purchase a small plastic oblong container that holds the wound-up cord and keeps it safely out of reach.

- For floor-length curtains that serve as room dividers, make sure that the fabric is not too heavy; it should be light enough so children can crawl out from under it if they get tangled up in it.

- Be sure the curtain rod that holds a floor-length drape is mounted securely and can hold your child's weight. You want the hooks or rings that hold the curtain onto the rod to give way rather than the rod to fall onto your child.

FLOORS

Whether they're lying, rolling, crawling, sitting, playing, walking, or falling, babies (after the first four to six months) spend most of their waking hours on the floor. It wasn't until my son started crawling that I realized how filthy my kitchen floor was—those knees, feet, and hands picked up inordinate amounts of dirt. I also had never been aware of how hard or soft a particular floor surface was until I had a child; then I became acutely aware of what types of surfaces were toughest to crawl on. There's no reason to get rid of a hard surface such as tile, cement, or stone once you have a child. You'll be able to make any of these types of floor softer by adding area rugs, or you can cordon off areas that aren't baby-proof or kid-friendly.

The tawny hues of wood add warmth to any nursery.

STONE, TILE, AND CEMENT FLOORS

Stone, tile, and cement surfaces are hard and can make for a nasty fall, but they also have positive points. They're easy to clean, keep the dust and allergens at bay, and rarely show signs of wear and tear. If you already have any of these types of flooring or a combination of them, you can make them more baby-friendly.

Place padded rugs over surfaces where you know your child needs a soft cushioning, such as around the crib or anyplace where they may pull up or climb. You can buy or make area rugs from unusual materials—cork, vinyl, wool, cotton, even rugs woven from fine plastic. These soften any surface, make the room less noisy and more cozy, and often look great, too.

WOOD FLOORS

Wood is probably the most common flooring in apartments and houses, and the easiest to incorporate into an overall plan for decorating a nursery. Because wood has a nice warm look, it fits perfectly with nearly all styles of décor. It has all the benefits of the hard surfaces without being as unforgiving. It's easy to clean and good for those predisposed to allergies. You'll want to cushion areas where your baby might pull up or fall down. Remember to use non-slip rug pads under all rugs.

Before your baby begins to crawl, go over the floor yourself. Make sure that the wood surface is smooth and that the cracks and spaces are filled. You don't want your little one getting splinters or cuts from sharp or rough edges.

CORK, LINOLEUM, RUBBER, AND VINYL FLOORS

These resilient surfaces are extremely durable, soft enough so that falls are not a concern, and relatively inexpensive compared to other flooring options. You can create a wide range of looks from wildly colorful to sleekly modern.

CORK Not only is cork flooring soft enough to roll around on, it lasts a long time and absorbs sound beautifully. Cork comes in three different forms: tiles (12" x 12"), floating cork (tongue and groove fit), and seamless cork carpet or linoleum. All of them are easy and fast to install, especially floating cork.

The better quality your cork flooring, the better it will wear, so make sure you look at a variety of corks before making your final decision.

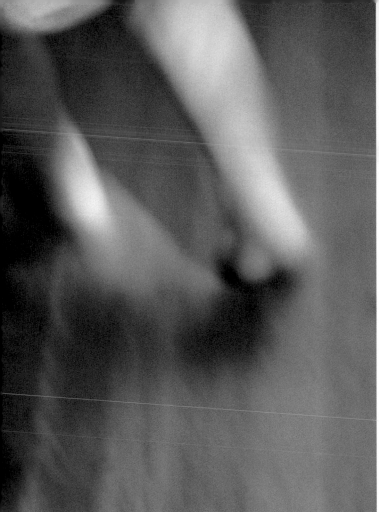

Painting Wood and Cement Floors

For a little money and a fair amount of elbow grease, you can add a whole new dimension to your nursery by painting and/or stenciling the floor. Imagine the floor a deep cerulean blue or a warm mossy green. Stenciling lets you create your own wild carpet of animals, trees, stars, moons, cars, airplanes, dinosaurs, squares, circles—the list goes on and on. Or you can paint the floor one color and stencil the floor boards or a border.

Wood floors have to be newly refinished or sanded so the wood will absorb the paint. Whether you brush on one color, or use stencils to create your own design, you need to apply a topcoat of sealer to both wood and cement after you're done painting. This will help to protect the paint from scuffing and chipping and make it easier to clean.

Stencils are available though catalogs, as well as at hardware, art, and museum shops everywhere. Also, look through house and design magazines and books to get a sense of how these floors will look when they're completed and how they will look with furniture.

OPPOSITE: A lively linoleum rug adds lots of color, is easy on little hands and feet, and is simple to clean.

ABOVE: Wood floors make the perfect backdrop for any decorating scheme.

RIGHT: Cork provides a soft, durable surface for crawling and toddling.

Because it's not naturally stain resistant, cork is finished with wax or varnish before or after you install it. Cork wears very well, but like any flooring, it gets nicked and scratched over time, so it needs to be sanded and refinished as often as wood floors.

If warm hues are what you want and wood flooring is outside your budget, cork is a cheaper alternative that's durable and comfortable with a nice bouncy surface.

LINOLEUM You can install linoleum in sheet form or tile; either way, this may be the flooring that's easiest to maintain. Linoleum comes in many colors, marbleized or solid, making it one of the more versatile flooring materials available. Linoleum is made with limestone powder, wood, cork, and linseed oil along with other resins and pigments. Because it's natural, it's a bit more expensive than its synthetic cousin, vinyl.

If you have linoleum, here's a tip to fill in any gouges: Take a piece of extra tile and make fine shavings from it, then mix with Elmer's glue and fill in the hole. Put a little spot varnish on top, and it will look practically new.

VINYL Any kind of vinyl you buy will be inexpensive, easy to maintain, stain resistant, and pretty easy to install on your own. You want to make sure that you don't buy vinyl made earlier than the late seventies, when it contained small amounts of asbestos.

Vinyl can take a lot of abuse, making it an ideal flooring for toddlers. It comes in sheets and tiles and is available in different textures and colors. Though it can be a little slippery for babies just becoming mobile, it's a hassle-free choice for parents.

RUBBER Rubber flooring is great for toddlers because it's practically indestructible as well as easy to clean, durable, and water resistant. It comes in an array of colors and patterns. But note that rubber is one of the priciest materials in the resilient group of floor coverings.

You can find rubber flooring at many dealerships specializing in floor-coverings. Most often it comes in tiles, but is also available in rolls.

WALL-TO-WALL CARPETING

Even though it's cozy, soft, and less noisy than other flooring alternatives, wall-to-wall carpeting holds dust. The type of carpeting you have makes an enormous difference in the amount of upkeep it requires. A high pile is more likely to get dirty and trap debris, and also wears less well, while a short pile or industrial-type carpet will be much easier to maintain and tends to trap less dust. Dr. Robert Eitches, an allergy specialist in Los Angeles, suggests purchasing "a very thin, very low, very tight Berber type of rug if you have to have carpeting. Of course, wood floors are a better choice for those who suffer from allergies."

Your child will spend a lot of time on the rug during the first years. Make sure it's soft.

RUGS

When choosing a rug for your baby's nursery, obviously you're looking for something that you love, that goes with your color scheme, or that speaks to you in some way. It's also got to be soft, durable, and easy to clean.

When I first laid eyes on the rug that I bought for my son's room, I knew that it was for me. I didn't have a theme in mind, nor were there particular colors I was looking for—there was just something very vibrant and lively about the rug that made it feel just right.

Obviously, expensive, delicate Orientals or Kilim carpets would not be the wisest choices for a nursery. Though they're beautiful, they can't take the wear and tear that a small child can dish out. Hook, braided, wool, or cotton area rugs that you can spot clean or throw in the washing machine will make your life a lot easier. There are plenty of styles of soft, easy-to-maintain rugs that would go well in any nursery.

Whether you're shopping at rug stores, baby stores, department stores, catalogs, or less expensive chain stores like Ikea or Target, there's a variety to choose from. You might like the funky, furry look of a machine-washable Flokati rug; the light, easy feel of a reversible cotton or chenille braided rug; the playful design on a hooked rug; or the colors, weight, and traditional design of an inexpensive Sumac or Dhurri.

The more colorful and patterned your rug, the less likely spots will show up. Plain rugs in pale colors will obviously show dirt more quickly, but if your rug is machine washable, or easily spot cleaned with soap and water, it won't matter. When choosing carpets, choose for love, but be sure you've chosen a rug that your child can play on without any discomfort and without your being concerned.

CLOCKWISE FROM TOP RIGHT: A plush, yellow daisy highlighted with a pink center adds a spot of color to the wooden parquet surface.

A medium-size rag rug brings the various colors of the room together and gives the space an even more intimate feel.

A hooked rug looks and feels especially cozy.

★ FINISHING TOUCHES

While looking for those final small touches that made my son's nursery, I became a kid all over again. I had such fun seeking out items that were whimsical, bright, and playful. It was important to me that some be found objects and some be family treasures—I didn't want everything to be new. First, I bought a colorful hooked rug covered with animals, birds, and fish. Then I hung a lively Calder-esque mobile that I had found in a museum shop, as well as a Chinese paper kite of an orange, electric blue, yellow, and lime green butterfly. Along with

them, I hung a collage my father had made for my son of a crimson-colored island surrounded by a black sky filled with glow-in-the-dark stars. I also put up a painting I had done when I was twelve and an Indian print that both my mother and I had hung in our childhood rooms. The other special finds were a vintage lamp of a little soldier and an old worn blue, white, and red rocking horse from the fifties.

Although none of the items mentioned in this section are necessary in a baby's room, each of them add to the personality and warmth of the space.

This fabulous thrift-store find was originally a projection screen, but here it's used as a fun piece of artwork.

TOOLS

- pencil
- small finish nail
- drill with ¹⁹/₆₄ or slightly larger bit
- X-acto knife

MATERIALS

- hardcover book, at least ¾" deep and at least 6" high
- clock movement mechanism, #118 for hands; if sweep second hand is desired, #S101 (see note)
- washer
- hex nut
- spraypaint to color hands

project: **Book Clock**

1 To find the center of the book, open the front cover and lightly pencil a large X from corner to corner on the inside front cover. The center of the X is the book's center point.

2 Score the drill point from inside the front cover by punching the small finish nail into the center of the X.

3 Close the book and gently drill through the cover from the front.

4 Through the hole in the front cover, place a pencil mark on the title page.

5 To create a guide for cutting the pages, place the clock mechanism on the title page, aligning the hole for the shaft with your pencil mark.

6 Outline the body of the mechanism to guide your cutting of pages, leaving a $1/4$-inch margin around the sides.

7 Cut on the outline using moderate pressure with your x-acto knife. Remove the scraps as you go. Keep in mind, the body of the mechanism needs to slide easily into the square.

8 When you have reached a depth of approximately $1/4$ inch, test to make sure the shaft can fit through the hole and the mechanism can slide into the square you have cut out.

9 Continue cutting out pages until the book closes to your satisfaction. It does not have to close all the way—you may want to stand the book up by slightly opening it.

10 Place the mechanism in the book with the shaft through the hole in the front cover. Secure it with the washer and hex nut, tightening by hand.

11 Spraypaint the hands of the clock as desired and allow to dry.

12 To mount the clock hands, gently push the hour hand all the way down the white plastic shaft. The minute hand then fits onto the rectangular post. Place the small cog-like nut on top and tighten (place it on, unscrew a half rotation, and then tighten by hand). Make sure the hands can rotate freely without touching each other; bend the hands gently if needed.

13 If using a sweep second hand, push the sleeve of the second hand onto the post with gentle pressure. Again, make sure the hands can move freely.

Note: The clock movement mechanism is available from Bradco at www.bradcoent.com, or call toll free at 888-236-8263. You can order the black hands to be painted in a color of your choice.

CHILD-SIZED FURNITURE

There's something special about kid-sized furniture in a nursery. Even though your baby won't use that small bench, little chair, or rocking horse for some time, these pieces give a lovely sense of anticipation, as you both look forward to the new experiences ahead.

There's a sense of mastery when your child can finally climb up onto a chair and nestle into it on their very own, or when they push their rocking horse back and forth for the very first time. The utter joy they experience discovering their own abilities and getting their first taste of independence is evident in the massive grin.

Look for small furniture in toy stores and children's furniture stores. If you prefer to hunt around, you might find something unusual at a flea market or garage sale. You can always make a piece your own by painting, stamping, stenciling, or even by doing decoupage.

OPPOSITE: A child's love seat and ottoman covered in pastel chenille adds a charming, feminine touch to this little girl's room.

TOP RIGHT: Kid-sized furniture offers toddlers a place where they can feel big and important.

CENTER RIGHT: This hand-painted stool serves as a seat, a bench for dolls, or a step-up to reach toys.

BOTTOM RIGHT: Toddlers love unconventional seating that's just their size—the apple-shaped beanbag is a favorite spot to curl up.

ARTWORK

To me, "artwork" means anything that you hang on the wall or from the ceiling for decoration. There are soft wall hangings—quilts, embroidery, flags, or kites—as well as more traditional paintings, maps, collages, or pictures. Artwork on paper can be framed or simply taped to the wall. If you're planning on framing, think about using a light plastic instead of glass or nothing at all on top of the piece. You want to keep the artwork as light and risk free as possible so no injuries result if the piece falls from the wall.

Infants and small children find any kind of artwork stimulating. At this point in their lives, you can hang anything you think is visually exciting, provocative, pleasurable—choose something you just plain like. There's no right or wrong choice. Look at how different the artwork is throughout the many nurseries in this book and be inspired—let yourself go. An earthy woodcut, a bright abstract poster, a framed piece of quilt, a vintage photo of family members—all of these can look great in a nursery. Remember that everything is new and exciting to a baby.

CLOCKWISE FROM RIGHT: A framed blackboard makes it easy to change a picture as often as you like; here a bright star shines for the night.

Bring the garden into the nursery with decorative butterflies.

Old or new, a quilt makes a lovely wall hanging for a nursery.

Colorful wooden animals brighten the walls.

MOBILES

The jury is out on whether or not mobiles are beneficial. Some experts say infants don't need more stimulation, while others feel that babies enjoy and learn when objects are suspended within view. Because most of us grew up with mobiles, many of us add them to our nursery for the nostalgia factor. Mobiles are a fixture in baby stores, and it seems for good reason, since many children respond to them with pure delight.

Mobiles are typically hung from the changing table or the crib for the first several months of your child's life. Some have soft objects attached and a music box that plays while the objects rotate. "Developmental" mobiles don't usually have music, but use shapes, bold color, and pictures of faces to stimulate your baby. (Because very young infants respond best to faces, these mobiles catch their attention.) The most important point about mobiles is to remove them once your child is old enough to pull and tug at them—at four to six months—so your baby does not become tangled in or injured by the strings.

Besides the standard nursery mobiles, there are some wonderful art mobiles that you can attach to the ceiling, which will swing and turn in the breeze. Unlike the mobiles that you fasten to the crib or changing table, this type can continue to serve as a piece of artwork until you and your child decide to take it down.

MUSIC

The part of the décor that you hear rather than see, music can calm you and your child. Having a small compact disc player or radio in your nursery is a wonderful addition. Watch how your child responds to music over time—at first with a smile, a tap, a clap, and eventually a whole dancing routine.

Whether you play different kinds of music all day long or use it to ease into play, nap, or bedtime, your child will take great pleasure in listening. And, as my husband and I learned, it's a nice treat for parents, since you will spend many hours in the nursery during your baby's first years.

OPPOSITE: A canopy of sheer silk frames the whimsical dragonfly mobile.

RIGHT: Soft, pastel-colored animals frolic with matching pastel balls on this delightful mobile.

TOOLS

- scissors
- tape measure
- pencil
- drill with tiny bits
- paintbrush
- large embroidery needle
- hole punch

MATERIALS

- colored paper
- 9 plastic baseball card sleeves
- 18 close-up photographs of familiar faces
- double-sided tape
- Four 18-inch dowels, ¼-inch diameter
- nontoxic paint in red, blue, green, and yellow
- 3 bundles (each 9 yards) of embroidery thread in blue, red, and yellow
- 1 yard colorful rickrack

project: **Family Photo Mobile**

Studies have shown that infants tend to focus longest on faces, so here's a mobile that introduces your family and friends to your baby. Although it's a little labor intensive, it's certain to delight both your baby and the people you choose to feature in the mobile.

1 Cut a piece of colored paper to fit snugly in each plastic baseball card sleeve. Then cut the photos ½ inch smaller than the sleeves on all sides so that the colored paper will frame the photo. Center a photo on each side of the paper frames and attach with double-sided tape. Slip the framed photos into the sleeves. Set aside.

2 With the tape measure, find the middle of each dowel and mark it with a pencil. With the smallest drill bit, drill a hole through the center of each dowel at that point.

3 Paint each dowel a different color. Dry the dowels by resting them carefully on a dish rack or roasting rack so that all sides are exposed.

4 Assemble 2 dowels in a cross by knotting the end of a 2-foot piece of embroidery thread around the center of the first dowel (but not through the drill hole), then passing the thread diagonally over the second dowel. Now pass the thread diagonally

underneath, then work it diagonally over, then switch to the other side of the dowel, wrapping them together with the same motion about 10 times. Repeat this process with the second pair of dowels, making sure that the arms of the crosses are even.

5 Thread the embroidery needle with about 36 inches of embroidery thread and knot the end. Use the needle to move aside the wrapped thread on the first cross, to find the holes that you drilled in the dowels in Step 2. Pass the needle through both holes and pull the thread through until the knot is snug against the bottom dowel. Wrap the thread diagonally around the cross a few times and tie it off with a slip-knot. Repeat the process with the second cross, leaving about 12 inches of thread between the two crosses. The remaining length of embroidery thread extending from the top cross is your hanger.

6 Using the hole punch, punch a hole near the top of each photo sleeve, positioning the hole in the center.

7 Find something like a coat rack to hang the mobile from to make this part of the process easier. Thread a 12-inch piece of embroidery thread through the hole in one photo sleeve and bring the ends together, positioning the photo in the middle of the 6-inch loop. Hang the photo by twisting the cut ends together and tying the thread onto one arm of a cross, near the end of the dowel. Repeat until you've hung 8 photos, one on each arm of the mobile, alternating colors of thread.

8 For the final sleeve, tie the thread around the middle of the bottom cross. To balance the mobile as a whole, simply adjust pictures by moving them along the arms. Cut off any excess thread.

9 Use rickrack to accent the central thread or between the crosses to make decorative bows.

STORAGE

When you first begin to imagine your nursery, you're probably not thinking about storage for storage's sake; instead you may picture an adorable toy chest, bureau, or armoire. These pieces of furniture are definitely useful, but often they're chosen because they add to the décor rather than for their functionality. They may fulfill some of your storage needs, but not all of them. It's very hard for a first-time parent to imagine how much space you'll eventually need for storage, but I can tell you that the nursery is an ever-expanding place. Between burpies, dia-pers, dirty diapers, blankets, sheets, toys, clothes, and dirty clothes, you are always looking for more spots to tuck or throw away something.

If you sort out your storage needs before the arrival of your child, it can help enormously. What-ever the size of your nursery, there are ways to max-imize the space, from an ambitious installation of drawers and shelves along a wall to simply hanging a mesh three-tier vegetable basket over the changing table. In this section we'll lay out your basic nursery storage options and suggest interesting ideas and solutions for finding more space.

Drawers are your first defense against clutter.

STORING DIAPERS

In the beginning your child will go through more diapers than you thought possible. (Don't despair; as they grow, they'll go through fewer and fewer.) You want to make clean diapers readily available without having them take over the room. Whether cloth or disposable, you can store diapers in the drawer of your changing table, in shelves above the changing table, or stack them tightly upright in a deep basket or box.

I found the basket method worked best for me. I was able to keep them neatly together, they were easy to grab, and they were out of sight. Plus, finding the decorative baskets was a lot of fun. Whether you look for interesting decorative boxes or baskets or decorate them yourself, it adds a nice touch to the nursery.

For the first four to six months when a child's diet consists only of milk, the diaper barely smells at all. But as soon as they begin to eat real food, the fragrance changes overnight and can quickly become a stinky problem unless you're on top of it. How you deal with dirty diapers depends on whether you use cloth or disposable diapers.

CLOTH DIAPERS When you use cloth diapers you're usually working with a service. The service picks up dirty diapers and delivers clean ones every week. They provide you with a plastic container to store the dirty diapers. Inside the container is a net bag that is treated with a bacteria-eating solvent that helps to keep the smell away.

The container often comes in a variety of colors, but it's almost always innocuous looking. If the container is not your favorite look, ask your service for the net bag, and tell them you will provide your own sealed container for the soiled diapers. If you decide to use your own container, ask the diaper company what they would suggest. The more tightly sealed your container, the less chance odors have to permeate the nursery and other rooms in the house. To help keep the smell to a minimum, rinse out poopy diapers; urine-soaked diapers have less of an odor. Note: Make sure your baby can't get into the container you choose once he or she begins to crawl.

DISPOSABLE DIAPERS There are three options for storing soiled disposable diapers: a Diaper Genie, a deodorizer pail, and a regular trash can with a lid. Both the Diaper Genie and the deodorizer pail are made specifically with the goal of containing odor.

The Diaper Genie works by compacting the dirty diaper and covering it in a plastic casing. You insert a special canister inside the Diaper Genie that seals each dirty diaper.

The deodorizer pail looks very much like a regular trash can except that the lid has a spot where you store a deodorant disk. These pails have a very tight seal to contain the smell and the deodorizer is constantly working to minimize it.

A regular trash can with a lid keeps the smell under control for a period of time, but you have to make sure that the lid is very tight or the smell will penetrate the room.

You can also store quart-sized plastic bags in your changing table to immediately dispose of poopy diapers in your outdoor trash receptacle, while using your storage container for urine diapers only. This will definitely take care of the smell and keep the waste problem to a minimum.

Since none of these storage pieces are particularly lovely, the best way to live with them is to decorate them as you would a piece of furniture.

ABOVE LEFT: Some containers will work now for diaper needs and can also be used months from now to store your toddler's toys.

ABOVE RIGHT: A decorative metal basket serves as an easily accessible place for storing diapers.

Built-in storage can be functional and add to the room's décor.

BUILT-IN STORAGE

Building in storage can be the answer to a big storage problem—if you don't even have an adequate closet, for example—or a creative use of an awkward space, such as a recessed wall or window. Shelves, cupboards, drawers, and changing tables are just some of the things in the nursery that lend themselves to a built-in solution.

There are wonderful ideas which combine both the utilitarian aspect with the decorative and playful. A built-in set of drawers can be imaginatively painted and finished off with fun handles. Use nontoxic paint, just for color or to decorate more elaborately by painting shapes, animals, or a landscape.

There are also plenty of ideas for saving space while maximizing it. Building a bench with storage underneath gives you a place to sit as well as a place to put things. Underneath the bench you can have sliding drawers, large sliding bins, or shelves. If the shelves are deep enough, you can place small baskets or plastic bins on them.

TOY CHESTS

A toy chest is an indelible symbol of childhood. As with cribs, no matter how advanced we become, the classic toy chest that your great-grandmother or grandfather used could be very similar to the toy chest your toddler uses today. And like cribs, toy chests are both functional and decorative. There are myriad styles at a wide range of prices.

The primary design differences—and what you might pay more for—are in the top or lid. If you purchase a toy chest with a lid, make sure it has a spring-loaded lid support to ensure that the lid does not bang down on your child's fingers or head. If the chest you have doesn't include this safety device, you can always add it, fairly easily and for less than ten dollars. In addition to ensuring that the lid won't close on your toddler, it will keep your child from getting trapped inside the chest if they were to climb in.

STACKABLE STORAGE CUBES

Whether they're wood or plastic, these cubes are a cheap storage alternative that hold an enormous amount of kid stuff. And as your children grow, they'll enjoy the freedom of pulling toys from the open cubes. There are cubes available that are finished, meaning they may already be decorated and fit snugly on top of one another. If you find wooden cubes that serve the purpose, all you have to do to make them stackable is secure slats of wood to the cubes so that they fit into each other safely.

The plastic stackable cubes are sometimes hard to find in baby stores. Try looking in kitchen stores, too. Plastic stacking bookcases can hold both toys and clothes. Note: Don't stack these so high that your child can pull them down. Bolt cubes to the wall if they're holding heavy loads.

SHELVES WITH PLASTIC BINS AND BASKETS

This is a cheap and amazingly efficient way to store toys. I've seen these units sold in stores such as Target and in catalogs such as Pottery Barn Kids. They are also very easy to make. The shelves serve as a frame for small plastic or metal bins, baskets, or boxes. The structure is low enough so that it's easily accessible to toddlers. It's also easy to relocate, so if you want to change your baby's play area, you can move it without breaking a sweat.

Bookshelves don't have to be for books until your child is older. You can use a bookshelf for stacking cardboard books, to hold bins or baskets, or to keep favorite stuffed animals in view. If you have delicate books that you want in your child's room but out of reach, try finding a cabinet with shelves on top, or mount a separate bookshelf high on the wall. Note: Again, it's important to bolt to the wall any piece of furniture that a child might pull onto himself.

LEFT: A shelf unit designed to look like a series of birdhouses holds books and toys.

OPPOSITE: A wall shelf that consolidates essentials can make your daily routine run smoothly.

WALL-MOUNTED SHELVES
AND HOOKS

Wall-mounted shelves provide a great place to store odds and ends. One single shelf can be helpful above the changing area for storing the baby's creams, ointments, comb, wipes, pacifier, etc. Several shelves or a small cabinet on the wall can act as a display as well as store items that you'd like out of your child's reach—from old books, toys, or framed photos to useful items like a thermometer, diapers, wipes, etc.

Having a row of hooks near the changing table can help you organize. You can hang clothes that have barely been worn or store pajamas, hats, and sweaters. You can hang a few outfits on the hooks in advance so you won't have to do a balancing act later while you're changing your baby. Between putting on the diaper and looking for something for your child to wear, you'll need all the help you can get.

Hooks or pegs let you hang the most-used items out of the way while at the same time keeping them handy. Whether you use them for outerwear or for bath towels, they'll become invaluable in your nursery. Just make sure they're secured to your wall properly.

STORING DIRTY CLOTHES

Some days, infants go through more outfits than adults go through in a week. You get so used to the constant sounds of the washer and dryer that when they're not running, it seems too quiet. I've become a big fan of the noise; it makes my home seem even homier. But you can't wash all day, so what do you do with all the dirty clothes?

For the first six months of my son's life, I used a basket. Then for aesthetic (I found an adorable replacement) and practical reasons (the basket was getting too small), I graduated to a hamper. Whether you use a basket or a hamper is really up to you. Some hampers have a laundry bag that you can pull out, which can make trips to the washer more manageable.

Even with something as innocent as a hamper, watch for safety hazards. Make sure that the hamper is not too heavy and that the basket does not unravel or chip when small fingers pry at it.

OPPOSITE: This combination storage unit lets you hang clothes from the pegs or display decorative accents above.

TOP RIGHT: A fun, pretty daisy peg is a useful place to hang clothes, hats, or towels.

RIGHT: A woven hamper keeps dirty clothes out of sight.

LEFT: It's easy to keep a child's room tidy when there's plenty of storage space.

ABOVE: Tiny T-shirts are more easily stored in drawers than closets.

OPPOSITE: Clothes and blankets are easily organized and stored away in this adjustable, shelved armoire.

MAKING THE MOST OF YOUR CLOSET

There are businesses that thrive on organizing people's closets. They can come in and transform what you once considered minimal space into a well-organized storage area. You can do the same for your baby's closet.

It's a good idea to begin by drawing a diagram of the closet. If you map out the dimensions and the configuration of the space, you can play around with how to best organize it. You have lots of choices of closet components. Will you use shelves, pegs, boxes, baskets, hangers? If you only have room for one or two of them, which ones will be most useful?

In the beginning, your baby's clothes are so tiny that hanging clothing is more cumbersome than useful. However, pegs along a closet door or in the back of the closet are wonderfully convenient for hanging hats, sweaters, shirts, pants, etc. For an inexpensive way to put drawers in your closet, think about getting mountable wire bins or plastic bins to keep clothing neatly on the shelves. You can also divvy up clothing and toys, putting away the ones that are too advanced, big, or small by storing them in marked bins on an upper shelf. Also, think ahead when planning closet shelving, leaving an easily accessible shelf free for shoes and slippers. It won't be long till they'll be padding around the house in their own little shoes.

Fun, Cheap, and Quick Ways to Store Odds and Ends

BASKETS: There's really nothing like a basket for holding stuffed animals, Legos, rattles, cardboard books, etc. The long, shallow rectangular baskets with handles are particularly helpful; they're easy to transport from room to room and your child will be able to pull his toys from the baskets unassisted. Smaller baskets are wonderful under a changing table to hold lotions, powder, diapers, etc.

CRATES: Junior milk crates are also handy. They're small enough to line up on a bureau or shelf and fill with practical items. Some people prefer them to baskets because they tend to be a bit sturdier, even though they're not usually as decorative.

BOOKCASES: Plastic stacking bookcases are a simple and affordable storage element for clothes and soft toys. Because they can never be as level and sturdy as wooden or metal shelves it's better to use them for lighter, softer items.

HANGING BASKETS: These may seem unlikely, but they work marvelously, and you might even have one sitting unused in a kitchen cupboard. A three-tiered vegetable basket hung from the ceiling over the changing table looks pretty and serves as a place to stow nearly all your changing items.

CHEF'S APRON: I've seen an apron with two or three large pockets hung above the changing table to store lotions, powders, and burpies—a fun and functional solution.

real nurseries

Now that we've covered what makes up a nursery and the various options available, let's see how different families created their own baby's room. We'll look at ten nurseries, each with its own style and story. Though each family has a different approach and each room its own décor, you'll find an overall warmth to each space. What makes these rooms special is not a particular item or paint color, but the excitement and love that went into creating each nursery.

FLOWER GARDEN

SHAE'S ROOM

Alex and Lisa had no specific look in mind when they began putting together Shae's nursery. Instead they decided to keep a completely open mind while browsing, trusting that when they found the right pieces they would know, and thus the room would come together.

The first order of business was to find the furniture. Since they live in a New York City apartment, space and storage were both considerations. They happened upon a natural wood crib with a gentle, wavy design on the length of the legs. Not only was

The hues, the flowers, the gentle simplicity of this golden space create a comforting environment.

it unusual, but the soft detail gave a lovely feminine touch to the room. Soon after finding the crib, they happened upon a blond wood changing table/dresser and an armoire, both of which had a similar hourglass-shape motif and happened to go perfectly with the crib.

Now that the essential furniture was purchased, the search for linens was on. Lisa felt that the linens would determine the color, as well as other details of the room. She and Alex knew that they wanted something bright and cheery. When they found the light lavender, blue, and yellow flowerpot-theme quilt and bedding, they "snapped it up," as Lisa puts it, with great excitement in her voice. "It was feminine without being classically girlie," and it seemed particularly appropriate since Lisa is passionate about flowers.

Even before their lucky find, Lisa had considered painting the nursery a pale lavender, but when the bedding arrived she and Alex decided that a creamy yellow was the way to go. After painting, they felt they needed a border to bring the rest of the bedding colors into the landscape of the room. They added an intricate, cheerful border of blossoms that united the floral theme and the colors they had chosen.

Details like floral throw rugs, flower-shaped hooks, a lampshade covered in daisy rosettes, a painting of butterflies and flowers, and painted flowerpots used as containers for changing essentials fell into place and helped to bring together the theme of the room.

ABOVE: A charming flowerpot-inspired quilt in soft, subtle tones completes the bedding of this nursery.

OPPOSITE: The soft lines of this changing table/bureau blend beautifully with the soft, delicate lines of the flower motif and of the other furniture items in the nursery.

CLOCKWISE FROM TOP LEFT: A fun, pretty daisy peg is a useful place to hang clothes, hats or towels.

Small hand-painted flowerpots are used to store changing-table essentials.

A simple lampshade with the addition of fabric daisies accents the floral, garden-inspired theme.

Windows provide the perfect opportunity to further your theme and color scheme.

A whimsical little trio of flowerpots makes up this soft, chenille throw rug.

A WORLD OF HER OWN

CAMILLE'S ROOM

When Christina and Jason moved from their Hollywood Hills home to Venice Beach, Camille Viola was exactly a year old. Camille had slept with Christina and Jason throughout her first year. In their new home, the family wanted Camille to have her own room.

Christina hoped to make Camille's transition to her own bed easier by giving her a room that was light, airy, and welcoming. "I wanted her to want her room," says Christina. Camille's room faced the garden so she could hear the babbling fountain, the chirping of the birds, and look out on the bright

The artistry of both grandmother and mother makes this little girl's room a garden paradise.

tropical foliage. Christina decided against a crib and opted for a twin-size futon. In the beginning, she fastened a bumper to the wall, but Camille quickly became used to sleeping on her own, and didn't need any extra padding around the mattress.

The futon has become a focal point of the room, a place where Camille plays and snuggles as well as sleeps. "She loves her bed," says Christina. "Sometimes she throws herself into the pillows, sometimes she rests looking up at the butterflies and the rose chandelier hanging from the ceiling." Christina and Jason also love lying there with her. "When you're lying on her bed you have to shrink down to her size; everything is at her level. It's her world, her domain."

LEFT: When toddlers are old enough to know the alphabet, they love seeing their name spelled out in wooden letters.

ABOVE: Children can rearrange the felt shapes on this handmade board to their hearts' content.

OPPOSITE: The garden outside is reflected in the garden within. This lovely nursery brings together vibrant color and imagination and is topped off by the painted wrought iron floral chandelier.

Christina decorated the room with this idea in mind. She wanted it to reflect Camille's personality. Camille loves hats, so Christina painted a hat rack and mounted it at the perfect height for Camille. She also painted a child's footstool that's just Camille's size. Christina's mother, an artist by trade, painted the wood molding in the room, Camille's armoire, and her small side table, along with the handmade wooden peg toys her father built for her.

The color choice for the room was simple: Camille loved pink, and it suited her little-girl sweetness. The walls, roller shades, trim, and the porcelain roses on the chandelier are all different shades of pink, which gives the room depth.

Each piece in the room was specially chosen or made for Camille, and every part of the room tells a story. Even the colorful sari fabric draped over the French doors was a gift Christina gave to her husband before they were married.

Camille's parents considered her tastes and personality when creating this room, so anyone who walks into this space gains a sense of the little girl who lives here.

ABOVE: An armoire painted with flowering ivy by Grandma makes this wardrobe completely unique.

RIGHT: A hand-painted flower gives this rocking chair its own personalized stamp.

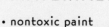

TOOLS

- paintbrush
- wire cutters
- pencil

MATERIALS

- nontoxic paint
- 30-by-3½-inch unfinished hat rack (available at most craft stores)
- large silk flowers
- craft glue

project: **Flower Hat Rack**

When your child has a rack this pretty—and at just the right height—hanging cherished treasures, hats, and clothing will be second nature.

❶ Paint the entire hat rack. While waiting for it to dry, cut the stems of the flowers to the base. Don't cut too close to the bud, otherwise the petals will have nothing to hold onto.

❷ Starting at one end of the hat rack, begin arranging the flowers. Mark with a pencil where you want to place each one. Put a drop of glue on each pencil mark.

❸ Adhere the flowers to the wood. Press down hard and wait until they feel secure. Let the rack dry overnight.

A ROOM FOR ALL SEASONS

ANNA'S ROOM

Several years ago, before Anna's birth, Debbie and Phil bought what used to be the ice house, built in 1850, on a farm in Croton-on-Hudson, New York. The land surrounding the house is full of spruce and magnolia trees, along with gardens packed with many varieties of bushes and flowers. This is a place where each season is reflected in the land.

Anna's room is the highest room in the house, and as Debbie says, "the most romantic room, a place where you can experience each season most fully." During the spring, visible from the the small window above Anna's changing table are giant, luscious pink

Open, airy, and *cheerful* are words that come to mind when looking at this quaint room.

magnolia blossoms. In the winter, she can see a sliver of the Hudson River; in the fall, ruby red leaves fill the glass; and in the summer, there's green everywhere. All year round, the sound of trains echoes through the Hudson Valley.

Debbie was seven months pregnant when they began to put together Anna's room. They knew they were having a girl, so they wanted the room to be pretty and light, but not frilly. First, they painted the dark pine paneling a pale butter yellow, with an earthy sage green along the trim. This immediately transformed the dark, slightly eerie feel of the room into a bright, sweet hideaway.

Several basic needs were already taken care of in the room. The vintage windows are so inherently lovely, Debbie and Phil didn't want to obstruct them in any way; luckily, they were spared the problem of too much light. One window has the original built-in shutters, while the other faces southwest, so it doesn't fill with light until the late afternoon. A small built-in desk under the window was transformed into a changing table by means of a changing pad thrown on top and the basic essentials tucked away in the drawers. While Phil and Debbie were fixing up the

house, they came upon a delicate scallop trim that had been used in the house at some point, so they put it to use as a decorative edge along the changing table and radiator.

The light maple crib and glider were welcome hand-me-downs that fit perfectly into the nursery. Debbie's one splurge was a light maple dresser to complete a trio of warm, woody basics.

As for the finishing touches, Debbie found two crystal lamps that had been stored away at her family's home. She retrieved them, dusted them off, and bought silk lampshades, which she decorated with rosettes. Phil's brother, an antique dealer, found a charming floral chandelier made of brass with three rosette-shaped globes. Not only did it go with the period of the house, it reflected other details in the room. Finally, a little treasured collection of stuffed animals from Debbie and Phil's childhood sits on a shelf: her Steif collection and Phil's favorite little stuffed creature, Lixie.

Phil and Debbie created a warm, magical nursery where the outside beauty fills the interior. Perched high in the trees with its dormer ceilings and golden glow, it's a perfect nest in which their child can dream and grow.

A small built-in desk with a multipaned glass window above it becomes the ideal changing table when a soft, cushioned changing pad is placed on top of the surface.

LEFT: The angles of the ceiling give this nursery an intimate, old-fashioned feel.

ABOVE: A childhood collection of Steif stuffed animals add that special, nostalgic touch to this little girl's room.

CARNIVAL CHIC

ISABEL'S NURSERY

When Sasha and Larry met, each had a child of their own, daughters who were only a year apart. Sofie and Eden became sisters easily and moved with their newly married parents into a sixties house that Larry had bought, but had yet to fix up.

Sasha worked her magic on this very clean, modern, glass home, giving it a fifties retro look with lots of blond wood and brightly colored items found at flea markets, swap meets, and garage sales. Though she had lived in both Craftsman and Georgian-style homes before moving, she was comfortable with modern design, having grown up in New York City in an apartment building designed by I. M. Pei.

Bright, bold, modern, and full of energy and charm, this little girl's room is made for imaginative play.

Soon after their move, Sasha became pregnant. With Eden and Sofie's input, she began planning the nursery. She kept the room itself very basic: white walls and curtains, with a beige synthetic sisal carpet on the floor. By keeping these elements simple, she could add color and texture as she developed her ideas.

The fun began with a flea market purchase, a 1948 Bozo the Clown album that came with a quirky picture book of animals. Sasha pulled the book apart and framed the pictures in sleek blond wood that matched the finish of the crib. Over the bed she hung a red-and-white canopy inspired by one of the framed drawings. The mock circus tent softened the look of the room, giving it a carnival atmosphere.

Many of the pieces Sasha found for the nursery served a different purpose before she reinvented them. Isabel's changing table was originally an old shoe display case, and the couch and chair were patio furniture before Sasha upholstered them. Even the spiffy shelves started out as an old metal cart before Sasha gave it a powder coating (a nontoxic process of painting metal furniture that doesn't rust or chip) and transformed it into clever storage.

Whether the pieces were found second hand or otherwise, each item was specially chosen for its whimsy and color along with its functionality. Sasha was clear from the beginning that the room would be fun. "I wanted the room to be festive and playful, a place where Isabel could have her own fantasy."

CLOCKWISE FROM TOP LEFT: Bedtime is more fun when you have a carnival tent to climb into.

The sofa has the same bold fabric as the tent. Pillows in a floral print soften the look.

The inspiration for the design of the room began with this flea-market find, a Bozo circus album and picture book, the pictures of which were taken apart and framed.

In this fun window treatment, the drapes are neutral and the rings add a note of bright color.

Long ago used to display shoes, this piece finds new life as a changing table and storage unit.

MADE BY HAND

GEORGE'S NURSERY

There are people who love to decorate and people who love to craft; and then there are those rare people who have both skills. Jane, George's mother, has that gift. In fact, both she and her husband, Bradley, found, painted, or made most of the items for George's nursery as well as the playroom he shares with his older sister, Frances.

They discovered their love of handmade details when Jane was pregnant with Frances and decided to sew curtains for her nursery. As she sewed, Jane taught herself some very complicated tailoring techniques. These curtains aren't merely a piece of fabric with a rod pocket—they're sumptuous drapes with a valance and piping.

Done in elegant, flattering tones, this nursery gets its warmth from the many handmade touches.

CLOCKWISE FROM LEFT: A simple, sweet quilt brightens a wall.

This handmade valance and curtain were where the decorating plan for this room began.

Toys on display add color and whimsy to a child's room.

The cushions of the glider are covered in fabric with the same motif as the valances.

Like the drapes, many of the pieces in the play-room and nursery have a special history. Bradley painted the changing table, a crackled Shaker shelf was a handmade gift from a friend, the curtain rods were copper leafed by Jane, the cow print has as its canvas an old movie projection screen that Jane spied at an antique store. The vintage prints of toys were a gift from Bradley's mother, who found them in a tiny shop in Philadelphia. Because the prints are so old and delicate, Jane decided to frame color copies of them, which worked beautifully.

When she began to put the room together, Jane was drawn to greens and yellows—a perfect choice, since the room is used as a nursery for both Frances and George.

Jane's philosophy of creating a home is apparent in every inch of these lively, comforting spaces: "Find one thing you love and go from there." You can't help but feel the warmth and energy that Jane and Bradley put into creating these rooms that their children love.

OPPOSITE, LEFT: An old movie screen picturing a cow graces the wall.

OPPOSITE, RIGHT: The colors are inviting and the toys within easy reach in this well-thought-out nursery.

ABOVE: The best playrooms offer kids a place to write and draw, to pretend, and to lounge.

GROWN-UP TASTES

MILO'S NURSERY

Before Milo was born, Laurie and Richard had renovated and decorated their classic Craftsman home with the help of an interior designer. So when Laurie began to pull together the nursery, she wanted to work with what already existed in the room. She wasn't interested in a traditional, cute nursery; instead, she wanted to create a unisex space that felt as handsome and mature as their home.

Warm, sophisticated colors make this nursery very chic and grown-up, yet the crib and suitable knickknacks make it clear that it's a baby's room.

When Laurie and Richard undertook the first renovation, the walls of the room were covered with years' worth of wallpapering, which they peeled down to the first layer. Using a technique where they painted cheesecloth onto the wallpaper, they created a textured surface that resembled linen. They gave the room depth with muted, saturated earth tones of sage and caramel.

Because it was a guest room before becoming a nursery, there was already a full-size antique wrought iron bed, a naturally distressed cream dresser, a couch, a sunflower mosaic side table, and a nightstand. Laurie kept all the pieces just as they were except for the couch and bed, which she recovered in white with lime green cushions.

She decided to cover the hardwood floors with Italian wall-to-wall carpeting in warm, subdued colors, which she felt "immediately made it an inviting, cozy little yummy place."

When it came to new furniture, her first purchase was a beautiful antique bamboo bar covered with convenient shelves and a perfect flat surface for changing Milo—this became the changing table. As Milo grows, it can have another life as a storage place for his books and treasures.

After the changing table came the crib. Laurie decided on a bold burnt red to complement the earthy, muted tones of the room. Then she chose an upholstered rocking chair with a rocking ottoman, again opting for vivid patterns and colors. These splashes of color add both depth and vitality to the room. Milo's nursery has an elegance that's on par

with the rest of the house, but it's got its own special ambience. As Laurie puts it, "When you close the door to this warm, inviting space, there's a unique feel to his room that's like nowhere else in the house."

CLOCKWISE FROM RIGHT: The warm linen-like appearance of the walls was created by painting over cheesecloth.

Small details, such as these beautiful boxes, pull the room together.

An old bamboo bar makes a stunning changing table.

Smart storage doesn't have to be dull. This cabinet, found at a garage sale, is a great example of function with style.

INTO THE WOODS

EAMONN'S NURSERY

Titus and Joanna's inspiration for this rustic little retreat was a set of woodcuts done by Titus's father of a bear and deer emerging from the forest. The woodcuts are beautiful, and represent the love the couple shares for the outdoors, particularly the woods of Maine. The rugged, wild terrain has always been a retreat for the two of them, because Titus grew up in Maine, Joanna has summered there since childhood, and the family now has their own cabin in beautiful rural Maine.

The tent-like covering on the crib, the wooden blinds, the handsome armoire—all of these touches give this nursery a rustic, cabin feel.

Creating what Joanna calls "Eamonn's cozy campground" came naturally. "When we began decorating the room we didn't know the gender of the baby, but we wanted it to work for either sex." They began by painting the walls and framing the woodcuts in burled maple. Joanna bought a natural wood crib and changing table, and designed her own bumper set. She found soft red quilted fabric that warmed up the room and didn't show any dirt. With the extra fabric, she made throw pillows, which helped to tie together the many red touches throughout the room.

Joanna's Swedish heritage played a part in the nursery. She made a cover for the changing table from a remnant of a Swedish rag rug. When she found a picture of an eighteenth-century Swedish bed that was partially draped by a canopy, she took the idea and made a canopy with a rustic look. (Note: A crib canopy is perfect for a very small infant, but not something to keep when your child begins to sit up.)

When it came to chairs, Joanna opted for a Mission-style rocker with a leather seat. Not only was it the most comfortable chair she'd tested, it also worked perfectly with the décor. For final, humorous touches she added a large moose-puppet head on the wall and a chandelier made out of antlers to give the room the feel of a real cabin in the woods. The antler chandelier was an afterthought—Joanna had ordered it nearly a year before from a hunting catalog and the light had hung briefly in their dining room, but neither Titus nor Joanna had really liked it, so it landed in the garage. When Joanna decided to use it in the nursery, she spray painted it red, distressed it, and finally placed tiny little lampshades over the lightbulbs.

As Eamonn became mobile, Joanna made small changes to his room. The canopy came down, and she made a special spot for him with a Lounge Around and the throw pillows she'd made for him. "He sits there for long periods of time reading and playing."

In this cozy, quaint nursery looking out onto the green trees, you're transported to a little cabin tucked away in a lush wooded area far away from the bustle of the city.

OPPOSITE, CLOCKWISE FROM TOP LEFT: In keeping with the woodsy theme, a stuffed moose adds a playful touch.

These painted frames are colorful and sturdy.

The mission-style rocker blends perfectly with the woodsy décor.

RIGHT: A soft, comfy Lounge-Round creates a cozy corner.

project: **Framed and Stenciled Blackboard**

Blackboards are wonderful things to hang in children's rooms. You can change the pictures often, and when your children begin to draw, they can decorate them by themselves. Framing the blackboard gives it a more finished look. It's important to frame it in a wide, plain wooden frame so you'll be able to paint and stencil easily. You can buy stencils, such as the Helen Foster stencils listed in the Resources section (see pages 150–154), or make your own by using paper and scissors to create shapes and scenes, as Joanna Welliver did to create this lovely frame. Unless you're very handy, we suggest having the blackboard framed by a professional.

TOOLS

- paintbrush
- scissors
- masking tape
- newspaper or clean butcher paper
- shallow dish or bowl
- sponge

MATERIALS

- 4-by-6 foot blackboard with a 2-inch-wide wooden frame
- nontoxic paint, for frame and stencil
- stencil (see Note)

❶ Lay the blackboard on a flat surface and paint the frame. Allow it to dry overnight.

❷ Cut the stencil out, then tape the stencil onto the frame with masking tape. Cover the surface of the blackboard with the newspaper or butcher paper to protect it from drips once you begin applying the paint.

❸ Pour some paint into the bowl. Using the sponge, lightly apply paint to the stencil. Remove the stencil very carefully and move to the next position on the frame, making a continuous design. Repeat until application is completed. Allow the paint to dry overnight.

Note: If you want to use store-bought, try the Helen Foster stencil, available at the Gamble House Gift Shop. See Resources, pages 150–154.

ASIAN INFLUENCES

MIA'S NURSERY

Hyun-Mi and David wanted to create a room for Mia that felt Asian, but not austere. With the help of designer Sasha Emerson, they created a nursery that combined Asian kitsch with the tranquil, minimal style associated with Hyun-Mi's Asian roots.

There were two things in the room that needed to be worked into the general plan. One was an enormous window covered by a plain rice-paper shade, which was just too expensive to replace. The other was a shelf unit that ran the length of one wall. Luckily, both were understated enough to blend in perfectly. In fact, by the time the room was done, the two pieces looked as if they'd been chosen specifically for the nursery.

Asian-inspired fabrics and lots of color give this nursery a hip, modern, yet truly feminine look.

real nurseries

135

Hyun-Mi and Sasha began by looking at Asian-influenced fabrics and chose a couple of fifties Asian prints, each with an American twist. Next came an enormous wall piece, which Sasha made by attaching hundreds of brightly colored fabric flowers onto a giant piece of felt with a hot glue gun.

The bright flowers became the basis from which all the colors in the room evolved. The walls were painted apple green and they chose bedding in a pale vintage pink. Hyun-Mi integrated the Asian-inspired fabrics she had chosen, reupholstering a glider with one and the bumper for the crib with another. The fabrics surround Mia with little scenes, which seem to delight her. "There's a swan in a lake, a temple—there's a discreet narrative going on that's stimulating in a subtle way," says her mother.

When the large flower piece was finally hung, it looked overpowering. So Hyun-Mi and Sasha cut it into three pieces and framed it in bamboo without glass, which emphasized the textures of the piece and made it completely child-safe. As a framed triptych the collage worked beautifully, adding color and a kind of pop-art funkiness to the space. To continue the floral pop-art theme, they covered the sofa in a photo-realistic poppy print. All the colors and textures work together to calm each other, making a fluid, serene space.

The final touches were a Chinese lantern attached to the ceiling fixture and hand-painted Kashmiri boxes that Sasha found at a flea market. Covered in hand-painted flowers, the pretty boxes fit perfectly into the cubby spaces in the black shelving along the wall.

When decorating this room Hyun-Mi found its girlishness emerged naturally. "I grew up in the eighties, when it wasn't applauded to be out there with your femininity. I want Mia to embrace hers. With her, I can reclaim all the great things about being a girl and a woman."

Common household items can be creatively converted into handy storage containers.

project: **Floral Tapestry**

This colorful wall hanging can be cut and framed as shown page 134, or hung as a single large piece. Purchase a piece of felt big enough to create a good-sized tapestry.

TOOLS

- pinking sheers
- hot glue gun
- glue

MATERIALS

- large piece of felt
- 300 to 1,000 synthetic flowers, in an assortment of colors (see Note)

❶ Using the pinking shears, cut the felt into the size and shape desired. The one pictured on page 134 started as a 6-by-4½-foot rectangle.

❷ Place the flowers across the felt, positioning them with an eye to color and spacing. Cluster them closely together for best results.

❸ Starting at the top left corner of the felt, select a flower and note the position of its center. Pick up the flower, shoot the glue gun on that spot on the felt, and return the flower to its place. Continue across the felt until you finish the row. Begin the next row, again working left to right, and continue until the felt is blanketed with flowers.

❹ Have the pieces matted and framed professionally, if desired.

Note: The flowers are available in bags at many notion and hobby stores.

OPPOSITE: A paper lamp, Asian artwork, and photo-realist fabric give this corner a pop-art look.

CLOCKWISE FROM RIGHT: Details like this pillow uphol-stered in an Asian-inspired fabric are the kind of extra touches that strengthen a theme or idea.

A detail like these table legs wrapped in the same bright floral fabric that was used on the love seat add a finished feel to the nursery.

Using Asian fabric as a mat for the Asian artwork, along with the bamboo frame, all combine to further the theme.

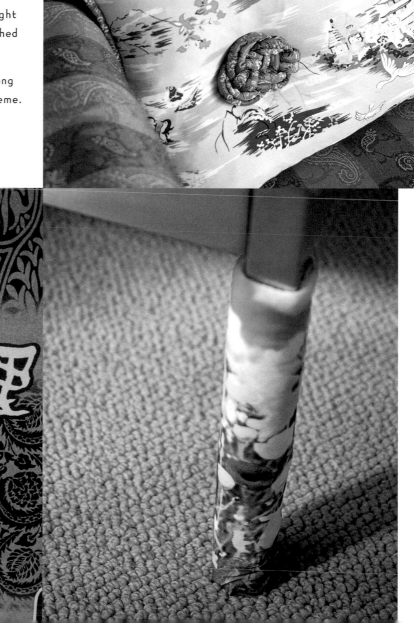

GARDEN PARTY

TESS'S NURSERY

Amy was six months pregnant with Tess when she began putting her nursery together. "I wanted the room to be old-fashioned, soft, and romantic, just like the name I had chosen for her—Tess Camille."

Amy began by painting the room an aqua color. "If the baby turned out to be a boy, I figured I could keep the room color and just exchange all the furniture." Amy went on a crib-buying expedition with her mother and aunt, who flew in especially for the occasion. As soon as they walked into the first store, all three women gravitated toward a gorgeous antique white crib decorated with tiny flowers and

Flower prints, light, and slightly distressed creamy furniture give this nursery a Victorian, garden-party look. You expect to hear the birds chirping and the fountain in the distance bubbling away.

bees. Amy admired it, but felt it was too expensive. Her mother and aunt wouldn't let her walk away from it. "They were completely indulgent. I loved it. I didn't have a choice but to say yes." When Amy discovered the crib could be converted into a youth bed and then a twin bed, she was able to justify the purchase.

At the same store, Amy found a hooked rug made up of flowers illustrating each letter of the alphabet. In her own room at home, she had an antique bureau decorated with a floral design. Amy realized that her dresser, the rug, and the crib were the foundation for a garden motif.

Other flower garden touches kept appearing almost magically as Amy worked on the nursery. While looking for an armoire, she came across a birdhouse bookcase in a shop window—Amy had collected birdhouses for ten years. The case was filled with linens, but she convinced the owner to sell it, and she happily placed it in the room.

An antique painted wrought iron plant holder from friends became a special storage spot for toys. Amy's mother, an antique dealer, had given Amy little vintage curios over the years, which now line the shelves in the nursery. Another special vintage piece hangs on the wall, a painting that was a gift from friends of the family. In it, a Chinese man is feeding baby birds, a perfect touch for Tess's garden bower.

"It couldn't be more suited to her—she loves flowers, loves the outdoors, is charmed by the birds. It's true what they say, a mother's intuition is a powerful thing," says Amy.

LEFT: These easily accessible bookshelves not only continue the garden theme of the room, they add lots of charm.

ABOVE: A string of fabric butterflies grace the wall above the crib.

A STORYBOOK NURSERY

ALEXANDRIA'S ROOM

Laurie had the idea for creating her own company while pregnant with her first child, Jack. She had run all over Los Angeles looking for things for her son's nursery and found it enormously time-consuming, unbelievably tiring, and often frustrating. As a result, shortly after Jack was born she developed babystyle.com, a Web site that would make it easier for parents-to-be by letting them order everything they needed to decorate a nursery without ever leaving home.

Soft pinks and greens and storybook themes create a delightful, feminine nursery that evokes a classic look.

When she became pregnant with her daughter, Alexandria, Laurie put her creation to the test by designing and decorating her nursery from her own Web site.

Alexandria's room began with toile wallpaper featuring the characters of Beatrix Potter. Laurie has always loved books and felt that reading was one of the great joys of her childhood, so these much-loved characters felt like the right beginning. The next addition was a window seat that looked out on the garden. (Note: It's a good idea to install window guards in window seats.) Laurie envisioned snuggling up and reading there with Alexandria, and hopes that years down the line it will be a quiet place for Alexandria to read and daydream. Laurie covered the cushions in old-fashioned floral prints, some vintage, some new, all of them in pretty hues of soft pink, sage green, and creamy white that are feminine but not babyish. She upholstered the overstuffed chair and ottoman in soft floral toile, keeping the tone and texture of the wallpaper. "Toile isn't juvenile—it will take Alexandria through till she's ten or eleven. I wanted some consistency in the room, a sense of longevity," says Laurie.

Bright and airy, along with being a perfect place to snuggle up, this window seat makes the room.

Once the fabric and walls were established, Laurie chose a crib and matching changing table, as well as a dresser hand-painted with delicate roses. All the pieces continued the timeless English cottage décor that fit so nicely with the Beatrix Potter paper. On the wall she hung pictures from other classic children's stories. Along with these pieces, she added a lovely ballerina table and chairs.

Both Laurie and her husband Michael wanted to add something of their own to the room, "giving a little heritage to the space," as Laurie puts it. Michael's mother gave them a pine dresser that she had refinished for his room when he was a child, and Laurie hung an oval mirror that had been in her room, along with a little rocking chair.

Laurie designed a classic, timeless room that has both a distinctive style and universal appeal, and was able to furnish it almost entirely from her own Web site. From the Beatrix Potter characters to the vintage fabrics to the cherished items passed from one generation to the next, it's a room with its own special story.

OPPOSITE: The painted furniture and Beatrix Potter wallpaper create a timeless English-cottage appeal.

TOP RIGHT: A detail of a ballerina adorns the special little table.

CENTER RIGHT: Mixing patterns—especially when you combine prints as subtle and delicate as these—can give a nursery a charming old-fashioned feel.

BOTTOM RIGHT: A vintage print of a small girl gathering flowers is in keeping with the theme of the room.

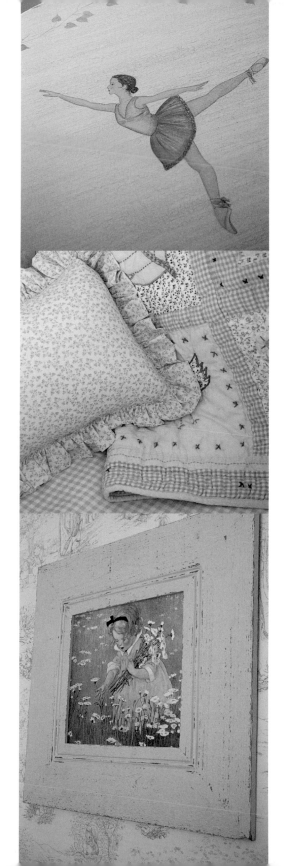

resources

LINENS AND BEDDING

Atlantic Blanket Company
135 North Road
Swans Island, ME 04685
888-526-9526
Hand-woven blankets.

Baby Rose
1913 Westwood Boulevard
Los Angeles, CA 90025
310-474-0444
Antique and contemporary
children's bedding.

The Company Store
500 Company Store Road
La Crosse, WI 54601
800-285-3696
Pillows and bedding.

DreamKeepers
10573 West Pico Boulevard, #354
Los Angeles, CA 90064
310-845-9106
(Fax) 310-845-1762
Imaginative bedding for children.

Garnet Hill
231 Main Street
Franconia, NH 03580
800-622-6216
www.garnethill.com
Bedding, linens, clothes,
and furniture.

Nilaya
121 South Jackson Street, #3
Seattle, WA 98104
800-208-4266
hilaya@uswest.net
Quilts and bedding.

FABRIC

Diamond Fabric
611 South La Brea Avenue
Los Angeles, CA 90036
323-931-8148
Fine fabrics.

F & S Upholstery
10654 West Pico Boulevard
Los Angeles, CA 90036
310-441-2477
Fine fabrics.

Michael Levine Fabrics

920 South Maple Road
Los Angeles, CA 90015
213-622-6259
Fine fabrics at discount prices.

UPHOLSTERY

The Home Collection

1605 & 1607 Robertson Boulevard
Los Angeles, CA 90068
310-551-6630
Furniture and bedding.

FLOOR COVERING

Don Blatchford Carpets & Art

1302 Montana Avenue
Santa Monica, CA 90403
310-451-9008
Carpets.

Linoleum City, Inc.

5657 Santa Monica Boulevard
Hollywood, CA 90038
323-469-0063
A vast assortment of floor coverings.

Westling

1308 Factory Place, Unit #11
Los Angeles, CA 90013
800-690-8007
Linoleum flooring and linoleum rugs.

FURNITURE

babystyle.com

www.babystyle.com
Furniture, linens, accessories, lighting, artwork, and rugs.

Baby's World

12348 Ventura Boulevard
Studio City, CA 91604
818-766-1100
Furniture, bedding, accessories, toys, and lighting.

Crate & Barrel

800-967-6696
www.crateandbarrel.com
Furniture, toys, and accessories.

Fun Furniture for Kids

8451 Beverly Boulevard
Los Angeles, CA 90048
323-655-2711
Children's furniture.

Ideal Unfinished Furniture

1018 North Western Avenue
Hollywood, CA 90029
323-467-3672
Unfinished furniture.

IKEA

800-434-IKEA
www.ikea.com
Children's furniture, linens, rugs, and toys.

Imagine That

8906 Melrose Avenue
West Hollywood, CA 90069
310-247-1270
927 Montana Avenue
Santa Monica, CA 90403
310-395-9553

13335 Ventura Boulevard
Sherman Oaks, CA 91423
818-784-8215

The Land of Nod

P.O. Box 1404
Wheeling, IL 60090
800-933-9904
Furniture, linens, bedding, toys, and accessories.

Little Miss Liberty Round Crib Company

270 North Canon Drive
Beverly Hills, CA 90210
310-281-5400
Round cribs.

Matter

4523 San Fernando Road
Glendale, CA 91204
818-243-2201
matter2@aol.com
Custom designed and
built furniture.

Mortise & Tenon

446 South La Brea Avenue
Los Angeles, CA 90036
323-937-7654
(Fax) 323-937-9022
Furniture, lighting, and accessories.

Nell's

7407 Beverly Boulevard
Los Angeles, CA 90036
323-857-6697
Antique furniture and
reproductions.

Orange

Marne Dupere
8111 Beverly Boulevard
Los Angeles, CA 90048
323-466-2497
Interesting room accents
and fifties-style furniture.

Pottery Barn Kids

800-430-7373
www.potterybarn.com
www.potterybarnkids.com
Furniture, rugs, and accessories.

Rocking Chairs 100%

212 Corte Madera Town Center
Corte Madera, CA 94925
800-476-2537
matt@rocking-chairs.com
Over eighty styles of rockers.

Room with a View

1600 Montana Avenue
Santa Monica, CA 90403
310-998-5858
Furniture, bedding, accessories,
clothing, blankets, and quilts.

ACCESSORIES

Baby Melt

7531 Sunset Boulevard
Los Angeles, CA 90046
323-851-7288
meltdown@primenet.com
www.meltcomics.com
Toys, comics, posters,
and accessories.

Beverly Hills Baseball Card Store

1137 South Robertson Boulevard
Beverly Hills, CA 90035
310-278-0887
Plastic sleeves, sports cards,
sports memorabilia.

Big Game Trophies

P.O. Box 4
Lyons, CO 80540
800-424-7695
(Fax) 303-823-9055
Decorative stuffed animals to
place on the wall. The Nature
Conservancy gets a donation
with each sale.

Cost Plus

800-267-8758

www.costplus.com

Accessories, baskets, storage, and toys.

The Cranberry House

12318 Ventura Boulevard
Studio City, CA 91604
818-506-8945
Antique toys, linens, and accessories.

Flicka

204 North Larchmont
Los Angeles, CA 90004
323-466-5822
Decoupage buckets, toys, clothing, bedding, and linens.

Gamble House Gift Shop

4 West Moreland Place
Pasadena, CA 91103
626-449-4178
Stencils, lamps, tables, and objects.

Hold Everything

Mail Order Department
P.O. Box 7807
San Francisco, CA 94120-7807
800-421-2264
Accessories, storage, and baskets.

Hollyhock

817 Hilldale Avenue
West Hollywood, CA 90069
310-777-0108
Baskets, blankets, pillows, and accessories.

Lily Henry Zoe

141 Barrington Place
Los Angeles, CA 90049
310-440-8150
Accessories, accents, beds, and storage.

Martha by Mail

P.O. Box 60060
Tampa, FL 33660-0060
800-950-7130
www.marthabymail.com
Accessories, bedding, and craft projects.

My Brest Friend Nursing Pillow

2525 Baker Street
San Francisco, CA 94123
415-883-5300
Nursing pillows.

NOVA Natural Toys & Crafts

877-NOVA-1111
845-426-3757
www.novanatural.com
Books, games, music, crafts, and supplies.

Ozzie and Moosy

5439 West Sixth Street
Los Angeles, CA 90036
323-938-8886
(Fax) 323-938-6886
www.ozzieandmoosy.com
Toys, furniture, clothing, bedding, and linens.

Puzzle Zoo

1413 Third Street
Santa Monica, CA 90401
310-393-9201
Stuffed animals and toys.

Target
888-304-4000
www.target.com
Cabinets, storage, and bedding.

WINDOW DRESSING

IKEA
800-434-IKEA
www.ikea.com
Curtains, drapes, and shades.

Pottery Barn Kids
800-430-7373
www.potterybarn.com
www.potterybarnkids.com
A big selection of curtains
and drapes.

Smith & Noble
1801 California Avenue
Corona, CA 92881
877-825-5555
Excellent window
dressing solutions.

LIGHTING

Cabelas Hunting Catalog
1 Cabelas Drive
Sidney, NB 69160
800-237-4444
Antler chandelier.

Fantasy Lights
7126 Melrose Avenue
Los Angeles, CA 90046
323-933-7244
Lighting and lampshades.

FRAMERS & INSTALLATION

Andrew Altamirano
1468 ½ Fairbanks Place
Los Angeles, CA 90026
213-250-5461
Baby-safe installation
for hanging art.

Beverly Webman
2922 2nd Street
Santa Monica, CA 90405
310-450-4448
b.webman@verizon.net
Framer.

Fast Frame
888-863-7263
www.fastframe.com
Framer.

HARDWARE

Liz's Antique Hardware
453 South La Brea Avenue
Los Angeles, CA 90036
323-939-4403
(Fax) 323-939-4387
www.LAhardware.com
shop@LAhardware.com
Antique and contemporary
hardware and lighting.

index